Cambridge Latin Anthology

Teacher's Handbook

CAMBRIDGE SCHOOL CLASSICS PROJECT

Cambridge Latin Anthology

Teacher's Handbook

Ashley Carter
Hitchin Girls' School

Phillip Parr
The Haberdashers' Aske's School, Elstree

CAMBRIDGE UNIVERSITY PRESS
Cambridge, New York, Melbourne, Madrid, Cape Town, Singapore, São Paulo

Cambridge University Press
The Edinburgh Building, Cambridge CB2 2RU, UK

www.cambridge.org
Information on this title: www.cambridge.org/9780521578547

© University of Cambridge School Classics Project

This publication is in copyright. Subject to statutory exception
and to the provisions of relevant collective licensing agreements,
no reproduction of any part may take place without the written
permission of Cambridge University Press.

First published 1996
10th printing 2006

Printed in the United Kingdom at the University Press, Cambridge

A catalogue record for this publication is available from the British Library

ISBN-13 978-0-521-57854-7 paperback
ISBN-10 0-521-57854-X paperback

CONTENTS

Preface   page   vii

Commentary: verse selections

Orpheus et Eurydicē (Virgil)   1

Nīsus et Euryalus (Virgil)   6

Ēchō et Narcissus (Ovid)   11

Baucis et Philēmōn (Ovid)   17

amor (Catullus, Martial, Ovid, Horace, Petronius)   23

ōtium (Martial, Horace, Catullus, Ovid)   34

vīta rūstica et vīta urbāna (Martial, Ovid, Horace)   44

dē cultū deōrum et vītā hominum (Horace, Martial, Virgil, Seneca, Lucretius)   54

Commentary: prose selections

Germānicus et Pīsō (Tacitus)   64

Messalīna (Tacitus)   73

avunculus meus (Pliny)   82

sāgae Thessalae (Apuleius)   88

trēs fēminae (Pliny)   93

persōnae nōn grātae (Cicero, Pliny, Sallust)   100

Druidēs (Caesar, Tacitus, Pliny the Elder)   108

tumultus et rebelliō (Tacitus, *Vulgate*)   115

Appendix A: notes on the illustrations   123

Appendix B: metrical schemes   133

PREFACE

The *Cambridge Latin Anthology* and this *Teacher's Handbook* have been produced to offer a fresh selection of Latin literature, principally for examination at GCSE. This is in response to requests from teachers and examiners who have felt that some of the texts prescribed at this level run the risk of being over-examined. It is hoped that the Anthology may also be of interest as a general reader in the first year of an A or AS level course.

The Anthology contains sixteen sections, equally divided between prose and verse and between extended passages and short poems and extracts. The choice of content has been based on several criteria: intrinsic interest, literary merit, accessibility and variety of theme, author and genre. Some of the themes are set in the context of the first century AD and are already familiar to pupils who have used the *Cambridge Latin Course*; others, particularly those of the verse selections, have a timeless appeal.

Because time is so short in many schools, the editors have tried to help pupils by reducing the linguistic demands of the texts in various ways. They have omitted difficult passages in the original texts and adapted the prose selections. In the latter, difficult expressions have been simplified in order to make them more accessible. Changes made to the original texts include substitution of a word or phrase, simplification of word order, and omission of material not directly relevant to the main story. In all cases, care has been taken not to distort the original meaning; where ambiguities existed in the original, these have been preserved. Every attempt has been made to maintain as much as possible of each author's individual style.

On the pages facing the text, words not occurring in the checklists of Units I-IIIB of the *Cambridge Latin Course* are glossed and a general vocabulary provided at the end of the book. Difficult phrases and sentences have been translated, often with an accompanying literal translation, and complex expressions have been rewritten in italics in an easier order.

The *Teacher's Handbook* gives a brief introduction to each passage, followed by notes on points of language, stylistic features and references in the text. A Discussion section includes ideas and questions that can be raised with the class. The Discussion is deliberately restrained and designed to be manageable in today's circumstances, but references for further reading have also been supplied. Notes on the illustrations are provided in Appendix A, while Appendix B contains the metrical schemes of the verse passages for teachers who wish to refer to them.

The editors are extremely grateful to the many people who have supported, advised and assisted with the preparation of the Anthology: Simon Boyes, Jill Hackford, Frank Hanbidge, Katherine Hedges, Manoj Jain, Scott Langham, Michael Lemprière, Roland Mayer, Isaac Moshe, Litini Newcombe, Richard Norton, Alex Panayi.

Particular thanks are due to the following for their editorial work: Alan Cornell, Margaret Flemington and Betty Munday; for scrutinising the text and making many valuable suggestions for its improvement: Robin Griffin, Professor E.J.Kenney, Pamela Perkins and Diana Sparkes; for compiling the general vocabulary: Patricia Acres; and for selecting and writing notes on the illustrations: Roger Dalladay.

Keith Dawson, Headmaster of The Haberdashers' Aske's School, Elstree, and Michael Jeans, Chairman of the Governors, are thanked for their support in granting Phillip Parr leave of absence to work on the book.

Two people have made contributions beyond what could reasonably be asked: Pat Story assisted with the selection of the texts and offered wise advice at every stage; she has been a tower of strength. Maire Collins has typed the whole manuscript with a rare combination of expertise and cheerfulness.

Lastly the editors wish to thank their families for their support and understanding over many months of toil: Margaret and Miles Carter; Bronwen, Christopher and Alice Parr.

Ashley Carter
Phillip Parr

COMMENTARY: VERSE SELECTIONS

Orpheus et Eurydicē (Virgil, *Georgics* IV.464-527)

The story of Orpheus and Eurydice is told towards the end of Georgic IV; it is almost completely self-contained as presented in the pupil's text and its insertion into the tale of the bee-keeper Aristaeus need not concern pupils. (The story of the pair is related by the sea-god Proteus: Aristaeus has lost his swarm of bees because he has offended a spirit by causing the death of Orpheus' wife, Eurydice.)

Metre: Hexameters

1 **ipse:** Orpheus was a legendary poet, son of a Muse and very talented musician; rivers, trees, mountains and animals responded to his song.

cavā...testūdine: the concave tortoise-shell had two upright socket-posts bored into it and a cross-bar attached to their top; from this, strings fed down to the top of the shell. An ox-skin was stretched around the back of the shell to help with the production of the sound.

2-3 These two lines are song-like in quality and should be read aloud by the teacher and later by pupils: the repetition (and the associated pathos) of *tē* in emphatic positions (*anaphora*), the assonance of *o* and *u* in 2 and *e* in 3, the alliteration of *t* and *d*, the rhyming of *veniente* and *dēcēdente* and the easy rhythm all assist the impression. They are very personal lines and, but for *sēcum* and *canēbat*, could be Orpheus' actual words.

5 The heavy syllables convey the horror of the journey. *cālīgantem* is a word as much of atmosphere as of colour.

10-17 Often the most fruitful approach to a simile is to ask pupils to gather correspondences between the point of comparison (the birds) and the control (the souls). Lack of correspondence can be illuminating, too: the birds will return to their old haunts but the dead will not. Here the principal idea is of number but additional thoughts include life and death, hiding, and migration from their old haunts in less favourable times.

18-21 These lines give an abbreviated traditional description of the horrors of the Underworld; those interested can be referred further to *Aeneid* VI. Ixion is offered as a general example: his punishment stands for those suffered by all sinners.

caeruleōs...implexae crīnibus anguēs Eumenides: the sense is clear but teachers need to consider whether to explain the syntax to pupils. *implexae* is used with an accusative of respect - literally 'woven with regard to dark blue-green snakes in their hair'.

atque...rota: Translate, 'the revolving wheel of Ixion stopped in the wind'.

22 Pupils will need to be reassured about the gap in Virgil's account (see Discussion). Orpheus was allowed to take Eurydice back to earth on condition that he did not look back at her until they had left the Underworld.

22-5 The lighter, more rapid metre of 22-4 reflects the happiness of Eurydice's return; with *subita* (25) and its elision with *incautum* we gasp at Orpheus' folly as the metre becomes heavier in *incautum dēmentia*.

27-8 As Orpheus stops, the reader also stops after the dactyl *restitit*; clues are given in *immemor heu! victusque animī* but the inevitable *respexit* is held till last word in the sentence. The unusual elision of *ibi omnis* positioned where it is suggests another gasp of horror.

30 fragor: thunder is associated with a sign from the gods, usually Jupiter, that Fate calls (cf. *fāta vocant* 33).

31 Notice how the question, clear and simple as it is, finds its answer almost accidentally in the vocative, *Orpheu*.

36, 38 The quick metre of 36, the slow metre of 38 neatly contrast the situations: she is whisked away (cf. *feror* 34), he is confused and hesitant.

42-4 The sounds and heavy metre of 42 are worth noting: they complement the meaning, for Orpheus is powerless. The end-stopped 43 tells us all we can ever know of Eurydice, but 44 with its initial heavy *septem illum tōtōs* tells us that Orpheus' fate will be just as hard.

47 These are some of the traditional tricks of those possessing supernatural powers and are easily applied to Orpheus' power of song.

48-52 The general approach to this second simile is that suggested in 10-17. The correspondences here are marked:

simile	control
48-9 maerēns philomēla… queritur	illum…flēvisse…ēvolvisse 44-6, querēns 57
48 pōpuleā…sub umbrā	rūpe sub āeriā 45
49 āmissōs…fētūs	feror ingentī circumdata nocte 34 raptam Eurydicēn 56
49 dūrus arātor	rēgem…tremendum 6, fāta 33
50 implūmēs	Eurydice is young and vulnerable: dulcis 2, miseram 31, invalidās 35

The particular feature of this simile is the quality of song of the nightingale: the vowels *a, o* and *u* offer a clear sound of mourning in 49 and the repetition of *e* in 51-2 gives a plangent and plaintive quality. The correspondence with Orpheus is obvious in the general sense and seen specifically in 46-7. Pupils should hear and say aloud this whole simile to appreciate its quality of sound.

55 Note the pattern made by the words in the phrases: **arva**que Rīphaeīs numquam **viduāta** *pruīnīs*. The pairing of words within the phrases is closely allied to the sense: Rīphaeīs goes in sense with **arva**, *pruīnīs* obviously with **viduāta**.

57-9 The idea of rejection in *sprētae…mātrēs* picks up 53: Orpheus rejected all thoughts of second love and marriage. Thrace was a centre of the worship of Bacchus; the mystic nature of the rites will be unfamiliar to some pupils, especially the ritual tearing to pieces of (usually) a bull, reflected here in Orpheus' fate. The essential features are night-time worship by females, lonely surroundings, revelry and drunkenness and wild ceremony.

61 cum with *volveret*, not (as pupils may be tempted to assume) with *gurgite…mediō*.

62-4 Eurydicēn: note the repetition of Eurydice's name to reproduce Orpheus' repeated call and its echo, even when (*tum quoque*, 60) Orpheus was dismembered. Although Orpheus would have called '*Eurydicē!*' (vocative), it was the practice to incorporate a quoted word into the grammatical structure; here accusative is required.

Discussion

One might approach the story of Orpheus and Eurydice expecting high tragic drama and it is certainly fit material for opera. Gluck's 'Orfeo ed Euridice' and especially the aria 'Che faro senza Euridice' could be introduced - and the work has a happy ending! Virgil's story, however, has only one speech of five lines instead of the usual exchange of set-pieces and the address to Pluto is simply not there. The drama and tension are of a different sort: we are not told directly of the famous condition given to Orpheus not to look back (will pupils know this?) but it is alluded to at 24, reinforced but still obliquely in 28 with *respexit*, and confirmed in 29-30 with *rupta tyrannī foedera*. Virgil is unconcerned with well-known aspects of the tale and moves the story on; he does this noticeably with *iamque* in 22: no preparations, just a departure already well under way, the metre assisting the meaning. The drama in 41-2 is of the rhetorical sort, reinforced by sound and metre; it is as if Virgil deliberately avoids direct speech in order to create more space for mood and atmosphere - and in these lines for pathos.

We can now appreciate the significance of the fast-moving story-line: it allows room for the development of colour and particularly pathos. From line 1 onwards we hear this in the song-like 2 and 3 and the expressive 7, picked up later in 26 with *scīrent sī ignōscere mānēs*. The atmosphere of 12-17 becomes progressively nastier as it moves through the pathos of the premature death of the young (*puerī...parentum*) to the horrors of Cocytus and Styx. There is room for contrast, too: this dark section is lightened from 22. Details are not absent: the pathos of *suam* (27), *immemor heu!* (28) and *heu nōn tua* (35) is poignant. Clearly the two similes play an essential rôle in establishing mood and colour. Significantly, Virgil spends thirteen lines of verse on similes, five on direct speech.

How fully are the characters of Orpheus and Eurydice drawn? We are told nothing of their backgrounds and very little of their marriage (*coniūnx*, 2 and *coniuge*, 41), although Orpheus' reaction to Eurydice's death and subsequent second loss suggests a great deal. Virgil is more concerned with their situation; he empathises with them. Virgil's attitude to Orpheus will be worth considering. Pupils could pick out the words of criticism in 25 and 28, then look for the words and phrases which make the reader sympathise (26, 38-9, 41-2).

Pupils' reactions to the ending are worth noting: some feel that the story just stops. It has been suggested by some commentators (quoted by H.H.Huxley, *Georgics* I and IV, Methuen Educational, p.198) that it is a weak ending, confirming the story as an insertion into another narrative.

Provided there is time (and it causes no confusion) Ovid's version of the story is a marvellous comparison: *Metamorphoses X-XI* (Penguin pp.225-7 and 246-7 or the verse translation by A.D.Melville in the World's Classics series pp.225-8 and pp.249-51).

Nīsus et Euryalus
(Extracts from Virgil, *Aeneid* IX.176-502)

Although the Nisus and Euryalus episode is largely self-contained, the pupil's text has a synopsis of the action of Books VII, VIII and early IX to help set it in context. Teachers will use their own judgement whether to refer to Books I-VI as further background; those with the time available may like to introduce this episode by reading in English the foot-race from Book V (286-361) in which Nisus and Euryalus appear as close friends.

Where summaries of connecting passages are given in the pupil's text it is suggested that teachers read to the class the full English translation to catch the breadth of the whole episode.

Metre: Hexameters

2 **comes Euryalus:** pupils need to note that Euryalus is somewhat younger than Nisus.

2-3 **quō pulchrior alter nōn fuit Aeneadum:** *quō* is ablative of comparison with *pulchrior*: 'and none of the followers of Aeneas was more handsome than he', *lit.* 'than who more handsome was there not another of the followers of Aeneas'.

3 **Aeneadum:** an archaic form of the genitive.

Trōiāna neque induit arma: the sense here needs *pulchrior* (2) to give 'nor did a more handsome man put on Trojan armour'.

4 **hīs amor ūnus erat:** *hīs* = possessive dative: 'they shared a mutual affection'. At some stage in the reading of this episode pupils will ask whether *amor* doesn't mean what it says, i.e. homosexual love. Virgil's readers would have instantly recognised the parallel with the homosexual relationship of Achilles and Patroclus and would need no further explanation. It has been argued that much of the emotional effect comes from the fact that the two were lovers.

6-7 **cētera...labōrum:** the setting of a peaceful, natural scene as a contrast before a passage of some tension is a familiar device in Virgil and other poets: while the world sleeps, some have matters of war to discuss.

7 **laxābant cūrās et corda oblīta labōrum:** *corda* is an object of *laxābant* and *oblīta* agrees with it: 'they were easing...their hearts, forgetting

their labours'. This use of *oblīta* is proleptic: the 'resting' will lead on to the 'forgetting'.

8 **dēlēcta iuventūs:** 'a picked group of young warriors'; the conventional translation 'youth' for *iuventūs* does not quite catch the sense, which needs to include those warlike enough for service up to 46 years. (cf. 29 *manus...iuvenumque senumque*).

12 **castrōrum et campī mediō:** 'in the middle of the camp and the open space'. Virgil intends us to think of what in a Roman camp would be the open space in the area of the *principia*.

13 **admittier:** archaic form of the passive infinitive.

14 The sense is clear enough; pupils will spot the indirect thought with accusative and infinitive if teachers suggest adding 'they said that...'.

16 **Hyrtacidēs:** patronymics may be unfamiliar. Ask pupils to consider the origin of surnames such as Williamson.

20 **portae:** as in 1.

21 Some of the watch-fires have gone out and are smoking. Smoke rising is not infrequently used as a sign of peace and inactivity - here rather dangerously.

23 **quaesītum:** this supine of purpose needs to mean 'to go to look for'; supines may well be unfamiliar (see *Cambridge Latin Grammar* 26.3).

moenia Pallantēa: the city was built on the future site of Rome.

26-7 Nisus and Euryalus have been out hunting in valleys and have glimpsed Pallanteum on its hill while they have been following the River Tiber.

32-3 **sed aurae...dōnant:** the pathos here is marked - see the discussion. The words prepare us for trouble in the pair's plan.

35 **inimīca:** this refers not only to the identity of the enemy camp but also to the fatal hostility it was to entail for Nisus and Euryalus. The latter leads on neatly to the contrasting idea introduced by *tamen* in *multīs...exitiō*.

40-1 Notice the number of monosyllables and disyllables suggesting military brevity and crispness.

46 **tōtō...somnum:** 'as he slept he snored deeply'.

8 Commentary: verse selections

47-50 These lines have a contextual puzzle: the three hundred are bringing replies from the city of King Latinus to Turnus to a message which we didn't know had been sent. We have to assume the usual relaying of messages between the leader Turnus at the front, attacking the Trojan camp, and the main body kept in reserve near Latinus' city (*legiō campīs īnstrūcta*) of which the three hundred are a detachment. It has been suggested that the introduction of the three hundred (a large number to accompany a reply) is something of an improvisation by Virgil: the poet needed a reason for a large number of enemy to chance upon Nisus and Euryalus.

53-4 galea...refulsit: this is the helmet Euryalus took from the dead Messapus (IX.365-6); Virgil seems to criticise his youthful thoughtlessness in *immemorem*.

55 haud temerē est vīsum: 'it was not seen for nothing'. The sense is almost 'they didn't need to look twice'.

56-8 The tripping metre of 56, the questions and the historic infinitives *tendere, celerāre, fīdere* all convey urgency and speed.

63 tamen intereā: Volcens means that, although he cannot punish the spear-thrower until he has caught him, his revenge towards Euryalus can be immediate.

65 ībat: the tense is significant as Nisus' speech accompanies Volcens' actions.

68 mē, mē: exclamations, outside any syntactical construction.

69-71 Nisus means that Euryalus was too young to cause any harm and came at his own insistence to accompany the friend he loved.

76 Virgil clearly has used the idea found in Catullus Poem XI; this echoing of Catullus is reserved for moments of greatest pathos according to R.D.Williams (*The Aeneid of Virgil*, Books VII-XII, Macmillan, p.302).

78 dēmīsēre: 'have been known to droop', the gnomic perfect.

86 Notice the finality emphasised by coincidence of ictus and accent in *dēmum morte quiēvit*.

Discussion

The whole episode falls into two parts - the enunciation of the plan and the speeches, and the narrative of the night-raid and aftermath. The first part is written in straightforward Latin 'quite without the usual density of Virgilian imagery and overtone' (R.D.Williams, *The Aeneid of Virgil, Books VII-XII*, Macmillan, p.291); it is 'slow and formalised' (p.297) and its meaning is transparent. The second moves much more quickly in a series of camera-shots, a strong narrative and ends with passages of great pathos.

The flavour of the Homeric world, especially in the first, is no accident: the episode is based on the night-raid of Odysseus and Diomedes in Iliad X which pupils may like to read in translation. There are many reminiscences of Homer's writing: Nisus is *ācerrimus armīs* (1), Volcens is *atrōx* (61); in the first English passage the individual hero's desire for glory in battle is set in a world where superiors need to be consulted in council; within the first summarised section can be found the thirst to emulate another's glory, the willingness to die and the redemption of a hero's body from an enemy; and at 24 we await the return of the hero *cum spoliīs*. The obvious model for the heroic pair of warrior-lovers is Achilles and Patroclus. More generally they exemplify the common Greek relationship of an older, more dominant partner with a younger, more passive lover. From 17 we know they are both young but it is Nisus who tries to protect Euryalus from going on the raid and who speaks first to the council of leaders; on the raid it is the wiser Nisus who lays out the plan and restrains the rasher Euryalus; finally the older warrior goes back in the forest to help the younger blade and passionately asserts the latter's innocence in 68-71.

The youth of the pair is not unconnected with pathos, a word which may need explaining to pupils. The idea of youthful death in war is clearly one which moved Virgil; the description of Pallas' death in Books X and XI could be used after this episode is read. Early on, Euryalus asks Iulus to take care of his mother should he not survive, an idea which prepares us for the final scene - and she is vulnerable, alone and unaware of her son's escapade. The first part ends (32-3) in pathos with the winds scattering Iulus' messages for Aeneas, foreshadowing the disaster. The second part develops and intensifies the pathos with the death of Euryalus and the lament of his mother, both ideas picked up and developed from earlier hints. Virgil's use of Catullus' flower simile seems even more appropriate with the crimson of the flowers reflecting the colour of the blood and the *arātrum* becoming the cold steel of death; Euryalus' mother utters the plangent cries of one whose sole comfort has been unexpectedly wrenched from her. Williams sees this as a rhetorically constructed lamentation but goes on, 'it achieves a high degree of immediacy, an impression of personal involvement which is largely due to Virgil's special sympathy...for youthful death'.

Our own sympathies move during the episode: at the start they are with the pair as we admire their courage even if we smile at some of the naïve speeches and youthful exuberance; their bloody and exultant massacre of sleeping enemies alienates us and Virgil's scenes are particularly nasty: see the translated passage on p.18; but we are finally reconciled to the pair when they are cornered and outnumbered, and when Nisus heroically but in vain tries to save Euryalus.

An interesting slant on this story will be given by discussing whether Nisus could have saved himself and whether he had any realistic hope of saving Euryalus. Pupils' sympathies may well change (perhaps more than once) during the reading of this episode; they could be asked why this is so - or why not.

Ēchō et Narcissus
(Extracts from Ovid, *Metamorphoses* III.356-510)

It seems that Ovid was the first poet to combine the stories of Echo and Narcissus. A.A.R.Henderson (Ovid, *Metamorphoses* III, BCP, p.78) notes that the pair are well suited - the one an auditory reflection, the other a visual. The tale contains much that will appeal to pupils - the saucy humour, the idea of unrequited love, the clever use of language. It is suggested that discussion with pupils of the verbal tricks should wait until the whole story is read.

Metre: Hexameters

1-2 **aspicit hunc...vōcālis nymphē:** pupils will need to be told that *hunc* refers to Narcissus who (in the immediately preceding lines) has just been described as the strikingly handsome son of the nymph Liriope. Ovid immediately catches the reader's attention with *aspicit* and a tripping metre but in typical fashion makes us wait till the end of 3 to find who is the subject. Ovid's adjective *resonābilis* explains and translates the name Echo itself.

4-6 Ovid is aware that his listeners are more likely to think of Echo as a disembodied voice than as a girl who can repeat only the last words she has heard. In lines omitted from this text Ovid explains that Juno inflicted this punishment on Echo for delaying Juno with idle chatter while the latter was trying to catch Jupiter chasing nymphs.

6 **ut...posset:** this explanatory use of *ut* means 'namely that' and refers to *ūsum*.

8 **vīdit et incaluit, sequitur:** the three verbs close together express speed of desire, followed by action.

9 **quōque** (not **quoque**) with *magis* 'the more'. This could puzzle pupils.

10-11 Ovid knows that sulphur ignites readily and at a fairly low temperature when exposed to a flame. Perhaps the poet intends us to think of the torches used at weddings.

12 **ō quotiēns...:** the use of *ō* is found in prayers and invocations to deities where the context is serious. Here it seems consciously high-flown for the situation and hence rather mock-solemn; it has a

gently humorous quality.

13 nātūra repugnat: because of Echo's speech limitations (2-6).

14 nec sinit (ut) incipiat: pupils are unlikely to ask about the syntax of this poetic omission of *ut*; the sense is clear.

quod (nātūra) sinit: 'what (nature) *does* allow' brings the reader on to Echo's only method of speech.

15 remittat: purpose subjunctive.

17ff. Here we see some of Ovid's best-known verbal pyrotechnics; there are broadly three types:

(i) 17 the repetition by Echo of the last word (*adest*) of Narcissus' remarks (*ecquis adest?*), where juxtaposition helps the effect. There are other examples in 23-4 and 28-9.

(ii) 19 the repetition in narrative of similar parts of the same verb and noun (*vōce... vocat... vocantem*) lending an echoic effect: the sound complements the meaning. The alliteration of 'v' here is a bonus.

(iii) 21 a summary reference to the words echoed: *totidem, quot dīxit, verba recēpit*; here the direct speech is temporarily discarded. Notice how Ovid sacrifices to neatness of language (*totidem...quot*) the inconsistency that Echo here repeats the *whole* sentence rather than just the final fragment.

Pupils are often amused by this once they understand the text.

23-4 coeāmus: the verb has clear sexual connotations. Narcissus meant merely to meet Echo; Echo had other ideas.

nūllī...respōnsūra sonō: '(Echo) who would reply to no sound...' *nūllī* as dative case will probably be unfamiliar to pupils.

25 Ovid means that she came out of the wood to make her intentions clear to Narcissus.

27 ille fugit...: Narcissus' refusal to be courted is attributed earlier by Ovid to *dūra superbia*.

28 ēmoriar: opinions vary on whether it means 'I shall die' or 'may I die' (future indicative or present subjunctive).

28-9 sit tibi cōpia nostrī: the sense changes between the two appearances of the phrase. With *antequam* the sense is 'so that you should not enjoy me'; without *antequam* the subjunctive is jussive, 'may you

enjoy me'. *cōpia* like *coeāmus* in 23-4 has sexual connotations here.
30 **pudibunda:** this could refer to *Ēchō* (nominative singular) or *ōra* (neuter plural) or both.
33 **cūrae:** this word is often used for the torment of love.
35 **vōx tantum atque ossa supersunt:** the heavy syllables and the double elision perhaps reinforce how little remains.
38 **omnibus audītur:** 'she is heard by all'. The dative is one of agent. Note the contrast of *audītur* with *vidētur* in 37.
vīvit in illā: the sense is 'remains of her'.
39-40 **hīc puer...prōcubuit:** 'the boy lay down here'. *hīc* is the adverb.
42 **vīsae correptus imāgine fōrmae:** the phrase is reminiscent of 22 (*alternae dēceptus imāgine vōcis*). In both situations Narcissus is making an error: the early one is auditory, this one visual.
43 **spem sine corpore:** 'an insubstantial hope' refers to the object of his prayers (the reflection) which has no physical form.
46 **geminum...sīdus:** the expression is a typical exaggeration of lovers' language.
47 **et...et:** the first **et** connects 47 with 46; the second *et* means 'Apollo, too'. Bacchus and Apollo are used as types of youth with free-flowing locks of hair.
50 **quibus est mīrābilis ipse:** 'for which he is admired'. *quibus* means literally 'as a result of which'.
50-2 These lines contain more examples of Ovid's linguistic tricks: the active and passive pairs *mīrātur/mīrābilis, probat/probātur, petit/petitur, accendit/ardet* correspond linguistically to Narcissus re-acting to his own reflection in the water and point up the paradox of the situation.
58 **quae:** the pupil's note (*quae = et haec*) may need further explanation. It refers to the appearance of Narcissus' breast.
liquefactā...in undā: *liquefactā* refers to the crystal-clear, mirror-like surface of the water after the ripples have disappeared; thus *rūrsus* belongs to this phrase.
60 **cērae:** these are likely to be funeral busts or masks.
65 **nec corpus remanet:** pupils may well go on to be puzzled that in 67ff.

there **does** seem to be a body or at least a person speaking. A possible answer is that in 67ff. there is a sort of flashback with Echo exchanging final echoes with Narcissus; this is clear from the mention of *caput* in 74 and *lūmina* in 75. *quae...ut vīdit* in 66 thus refers to Echo watching the process before it fin͟ished, with only the *corpus* left. An alternative would be to have 65 mean 'but it was not the physique which Echo had once loved'; in other words the *corpus* was a hollow shell. With this interpretation, *quae* in 66 could refer to Echo, 'she', and death comes in the due order of things in 75.

Notice the way in which Ovid now weaves Echo back into the story: Narcissus' fate is similar to that of Echo. The technique gives shape to the joining of the separate stories. In view of the note above one may feel Ovid's efforts are not entirely successful.

- 67-9 **quotiēns...dīxerat; cum...percusserat:** the pluperfect is used for repeated actions, 'whenever he said... hit'.
- 72 **dīlēcte:** the vocative of *dīlēctus* will need comment.
- 72-3 **totidem...Ēchō:** Henderson (p.91) notes that Ovid is playing with the two ideas of echoes: the naturally occurring ones (*totidem remīsit verba locus*) and the responses of Echo the nymph (*inquit et Ēchō*). This is Ovid's wit at work. Pupils may like to know that Ovid's text as it was read in antiquity did not distinguish small and capital letters; readers were not directed to echo the natural phenomenon or Echo the nymph but could understand both at once.
- 77-9 **plānxēre...plānxērunt...plangentibus:** the plangent sounds complement the meaning.
  sorōrēs...Nāides...Dryades: Narcissus' mother was a nymph.
- 78 **sectōs...capillōs:** hair was cut in mourning and given as an offering (*posuēre*) to the dead.
- 80 **quassāsque facēs:** the meaning required is 'torches that are shaken at funerals'.

Discussion

If Ovid gives us a tragedy in the stories of Echo and Narcissus then it is likely to be found in the circumstances which manage to keep apart two seemingly ideally-suited young people. The situation in which girl chases boy will not be lost on pupils; it is, too, the opposite of the usual in Ovid where god chases nymph. Pupils will be puzzled that Narcissus summarily rejects Echo's advances and few clues are given in the text presented. In the earlier omitted part of the story Narcissus' behaviour is attributed to *dūra superbia* and it extends to rejection of male admirers. However, in 41ff. we find that Narcissus does love another and he is male. It is important to remember that the reader knows the identity of the face in the water: the focus of interest in the story is not the homosexual nature of Narcissus' feelings but their self-directedness. The question of sexuality will need to be addressed at some stage in the discussion but we should remember that attitudes in the ancient world towards homosexuality were different from those of today. It is suggested that too much emphasis on this theme will detract from the overall appreciation of the story. The poet, incidentally, does not allow the narrative to become diffused by elaborately explaining why Narcissus reached the age of 16 without having seen his reflection in water; this is acknowledged, however, in an apostrophe to Narcissus omitted from this selection.

The character of Echo is more fleetingly drawn. She is roughly treated but it is not she who utters the curse on Narcissus (referred to in the summary in the pupil's text). Echo is essentially nymph-like: young, vulnerable and playful. If the eventual fate of Narcissus mirrors that of Echo, it is not of her making; indeed, she seems to show compassion (79: *plangentibus assonat Ēchō*). Ovid is more interested in the character of Narcissus and his interest leads him to over-emphasise some ideas, for example the elusiveness of the lover in the section given in translation in the pupil's text. Henderson (p.83) sees Ovid's intention as to create pathos: 'we are invited to shake our heads sadly over the simple-mindedness of the poor youth' (cf.43 *corpus...est*; 51 *imprūdēns*; 56 *quid videat nescit*; 57 *dēcipit...error*). The active/passive correspondences in 50-2 are a skilful technique to invite us to examine Narcissus' thought-processes, even if they are centred around the feelings of Narcissus the lover but not the feelings of Narcissus the beloved.

But it would be wrong to view the story too seriously, as a passionate tragedy. Ovid's lightness of touch is underpinned by vocabulary owing more to love-poetry (52 *petere, accendere, ardēre*; 56 *ūrī*; 62 *carpī*); and the witty *in Stygiā spectābat aquā* (77) is significant. It will be interesting to see how spontaneously pupils respond to the verbal tricks which assist the tone so fundamentally. In addition to those referred to in the notes, consider too 27 the juxtaposition of *fugit fugiēns*; 41-2 the word patterning based around *dumque* and *sitis*; 67-8 *ēheu* repeated; 73 the repetition of *valē* with differing metrical quantities: *valē, vale*. It is no coincidence that, with one exception only, Ovid leaves mention of Echo's name till last word in the line where maximum emphasis is given to her echoic quality. Such verbal artistry will be fully appreciated only if the Latin is read aloud to the pupils.

Pupils will ask about metamorphosis in Ovid's work. Here the process of metamorphosis, so often explored by Ovid, can be better observed in Echo's change of body into nothing but beautiful auditory reflection (33-6) and stone (36); by contrast, Narcissus' fate is somewhat less clearly defined because it seems to come in two stages (see note on 65): there is the dissolution of his body followed later by the simple result (but not the process) of his metamorphosis into a flower. For both Echo and Narcissus, metamorphosis allows death to be side-stepped: their existence continues in a different form.

Pupils will enjoy discussing which of the two characters (and why) it is easier to sympathise with. Likewise a useful comparison can be made between the similes in 10-11, 44-5 (and the end of the translation on p.32); is any of them more effective or striking than the others?

Baucis et Philēmōn
(Ovid, *Metamorphoses* VIII.626-719)

The story of Baucis and Philemon is one of several tales related after dinner to a group of heroes in the cave of the river god Achelous. Pirithous is contemptuous of the power of the gods and the elderly Lelex relates this tale to show that he should have more respect. The Achelous episode begins on p.194 of the Penguin translation and ends on p.205; there are several stories here which expand upon the general theme of the gods' power.

Metre: Hexameters

2 **Atlantiadēs:** Atlas was the father of Maia who became by Jupiter the mother of Mercury.

positīs cādūcifer ālīs: the *cādūceus* or herald's staff was appropriate for Mercury as messenger of the gods. *cādūcifer* is used as a stock description of Mercury: he cannot for dramatic reasons have the staff with him. *ālīs* refers to the wings on Mercury's sandals or helmet.

3-4 **mīlle domōs adiēre...mīlle domōs clausēre:** Ovid is fond of patterns of word and sound. The house is referred to later (8) as *casa* and may be imagined as little more than a shack, with a low door, as line 13 makes clear. The low door would allow in small animals such as the goose (41) but deter larger animals. The house would probably have a hole in the thatched roof for ventilation and the smoky interior would allow meat to be cured hanging from the rafters (cf.22ff.). Pupils could draw the exterior of the cottage as an aide-mémoire; this could stimulate comparison with living conditions of the wealthy.

6 **pia:** the dutifulness of Baucis and, by implication, of Philemon is a recurrent theme of the tale; it contrasts with the *impia vīcīnia* of 46-7.

7-11 There are several examples of word and sound patterning here: *illā...illā; cōnsenuēre...effēcēre; fatendō...ferendō; dominōs... famulōs; pārentque...iubentque.* Once the meaning is clear pupils can be invited to speculate on Ovid's intentions and whether there are parallels in English poetry. An example can be found in number five of *Five Songs* by W.H.Auden:

'O where are you going?' said reader to rider,
'That valley is fatal when furnaces burn,
Yonder's the midden whose odours will madden,
That gap is the grave where the tall return.'

and in *Arms and the Boy* by Wilfred Owen:

Let the boy try along this bayonet-blade
How cold steel is, and keen with hunger of blood;
Blue with all malice, like a madman's flash;
And thinly drawn with famishing for flesh.

and in the poetry of Baudelaire, where associative sounds are often to be found:

Il est amer et doux, pendant les nuits d'hiver,
D'écouter, près du feu qui palpite et qui fume,
Les souvenirs lointains lentement s'élever
Au bruit des carillons qui chantent dans la brume.
                          (*La Cloche Fêlée* from *Les Fleurs du Mal*)

10 **rēfert:** this is the impersonal verb (not *refert*) - 'it matters', 'it makes a difference'.

10-11 The gentle humour first seen here is a feature of the whole episode.

12 **caelicolae:** we the readers are reminded of the greatness of the guests in this epic-sounding word. The effect is heightened by its juxtaposition with *parvōs* and by the guests needing to stoop to enter the hut.

15 **sēdula:** the word nicely captures the picture of someone bustling around trying to do her best for unexpected guests.

18 **ad flammās animā prōdūcit anīlī:** this phrase, difficult to translate literally, refers to Baucis' blowing on the leaves and bark to ignite them - 'she blew on them with an old woman's breath to make them catch light'.

19-20 Baucis gathers small pieces of kindling, stored inside the roof-space to keep them dry - not from the outside of the roof, as pupils sometimes think - and splits them still further as an economy measure, or perhaps just to assist the process of catching fire.

22 **truncat holus foliīs:** either the outer leaves of a cabbage or the stripping of something like spinach. Translate, 'she strips the vegetables of their leaves'.

23 **sordida terga suis nigrō pendentia tignō:** pork, the diet of poorer Italians, was salted and hung up to be smoked. *suis* will need careful identification to distinguish from *suīs*. *terga* (from *tergum*) and the rarer word *tergore* (24) (from *tergus*) may confuse pupils since they are used close together.

24-5 **servātō...diū...partem exiguam:** more honest economy.

27-30 **erat alveus...artūsque fovendōs accipit:** the natural interpretation would have the gods wash themselves in warm water provided by the hosts; it has been suggested by Hollis (Ovid, *Metamorphoses* VIII, OUP, pp.117-18), that the hosts wash the feet of their guests as a gesture of hospitality. There are several examples from Greek literature and the Bible.

clāvō suspēnsus ab ānsā: 'hung up by its handle from a nail'.

34 **vestis...lectō nōn indignanda salignō:** more gentle humour. Presumably willow was plentiful, gathered locally and easily worked; it had as little special value as the cloth spread over the couch.

English section: the food is simple and, apart from the pork, vegetarian - giving a firm Italian context. The olives, radish, cheese, eggs etc. are the *gustātiō*, followed by wine in (more humour) no silver (i.e. earthenware) cups; then comes the main course of hot food, followed by wine; and finally the dessert of nuts and fruit. The wine is brought out and removed between courses.

36 **crātēra:** heavy sweet wine was mixed in variable proportions with water in a mixing-bowl before being served in cups. The miracle leads to recognition, or at least suspicion, of the guests as divinities.

38 **manibus...supīnīs:** palms upturned were the ancient Roman posture of prayer. This further evidence of recognition is accompanied by vocabulary such as *precēs* (39), *timidus* (39), *ad ipsōs...deōs* (44-5). The confirmation of the old people's suspicion comes in 46: *dī...sumus*.

39 timidus: qualifies both Baucis and Philemon.

43-5 The humorous scene of the old pair scurrying around to catch the flapping goose is endearing; the goose, too, seems to recognise the gods and, paradoxically in a way, flies to them for sanctuary: he was to have been their next course!

45 superī vetuēre necārī: pupils need to realise that the gods do not want the goose killed and are satisfied with the hospitality.

46ff. The idea of a flood as a punishment for men's wickedness with one man and his family surviving may be familiar to pupils from the Bible and the idea goes wider in the Middle East. There is the opportunity for some cooperation with the religious education department in teaching this section. Pupils may like to read Ovid's other flood story, Deucalion and Pyrrha, in the Penguin translation pp.34ff. The idea of revenge or retribution by the gods is powerful throughout the *Metamorphoses* (cf.*impia* (47) and *pia* (6)).

vīcīnia...impia: may need explanation with reference to 3-4.

51 The metre is long and slow to reflect the couple's effort up the slope.

52-3 They were a bow-shot's distance from the summit.

56ff. This is a secondary metamorphosis within the story, presumably intended to honour the spot where hospitality was offered. Pupils should be guided away from any idea of punishment.

57 furcās: these are the fork-shaped gable-supports of the cottage.

58 tēcta videntur: 'the roof is seen to be...'.

59 caelātae...forēs: the doors were most likely of bronze with relief work.

60 Saturn is equated in Greek mythology with Cronos, father of Zeus.

60-2 The tone becomes more epic and solemn as the gods prepare to reward the couple: notice the formality of 60 and of the address in 61-2.

pauca locūtus: offers us the touching picture of the couple conferring and brings us back to their simple world.

63 iūdicium...commūne: this reminds us of their unanimity in 11.

65 concordēs...annōs: the idea of togetherness is continued and extends to their request to die together.

66-7 auferat...videam...sim: jussive subjunctives, especially in these difficult lines, will need help: 'let the same hour carry off the two of us and let me never see the tomb of my wife and may I not have to be buried by her'.

68 vōta fidēs sequitur: 'fulfilment of the request followed', literally 'fulfilment followed the prayers'. The contractual nature of the *vōtum* has already been fulfilled on Baucis' and Philemon's part by their dutifulness; the gods now fulfil their part.

68-9 Ovid, in a familiar device, moves the story quickly on to the finale of the metamorphosis: we hear little of the couple's service.

71-2 frondēre Philēmona Baucis: the abruptness of this is surely intended to be humorous. People changing into trees (or birds) is the most common metamorphosis in Ovid's work. The reader is often treated to a step-by-step description of bark and foliage spreading up over the body and face with the mouth being the last part to be affected - here in 73 and 75-6. The final word *coniūnx* with its sense of 'joining' has a special value in this story. Teachers may like to read in translation for purposes of comparison the story of the transformation of the Heliades, Penguin p.59.

75-6 'The sibilants of the Latin suggest the rustling of the miraculously burgeoning leaves' (E.J.Kenney in the A.D.Melville translation, p.424, World's Classics, OUP).

Discussion

The definitive commentary by Hollis outlines a host of various strands which come together with this story: there are Greek, Near Eastern, Middle Eastern and Italian elements. It seems that Ovid was the first to tell the story in this finished form.

There is much that can be compared with ideas familiar to pupils from religious education: the theme of gods coming down to earth to visit men is so familiar in Greek mythology that pupils may not think to extend it towards similarities in the New Testament, e.g. the failure to recognise divinity. An interesting parallel to the present story is found in *Acts of the Apostles* where Paul and Barnabas are identified at Lystra in Galatia as

Jupiter and Mercury ('The gods have come down to us in the likeness of men.' *Acts* 14,11). In our story this failure is dramatically important since it underscores the simplicity of Baucis and Philemon. Their hospitality to strangers is typical of the ancient ideal and even today far more familiar to the peoples of the eastern Mediterranean than it is to us further west; this is essentially a simple tale of hospitality, piety and reward and the story of Erysichthon which follows provides a foil for it.

Much can be made of the moral theme and it certainly fits in with ideas, prevalent at the time of Ovid's writing, of the moral regeneration of Rome under Augustus; however, this will be better known to teachers than pupils and over-emphasis will obscure the simplicity of the story. Nevertheless it is clear that our couple are Italian peasant stock of a type, albeit idealised, which found favour not least in poetry of the period: they have lived in the same cottage all their lives, are blissfully united, are content with little and have no trappings of wealth, show traditional hospitality and respect the gods. How will this appeal to today's pupils?

Why does Ovid tell the tale? If there is, as some have seen, a heavy moral quasi-political message then it certainly jars against much of the rest of his work. No, the story provided Ovid's fertile mind with the opportunity to combine disparate strands into one story in an Italian setting and to exploit the humour of the situation, albeit in a gentle and respectful way. Besides this, we should not deny any religious respect to the writer, although in fact this story is not particularly religious but rather concerns decency and goodness.

Discussion with pupils can centre on disentangling the four elements of the old people's morality: indifference to riches, hospitality to strangers, mutual affection, piety to the gods. When they have detected the humour, they might consider whether it detracts from the moral theme; if Ovid is making fun of Baucis and Philemon, does that mean he is making fun of poverty, hospitality, conjugal love and piety? Indeed, some may feel that the humour actually strengthens the moral theme by humanising it.

amor

How many kisses? (Catullus, *Poem 7*)

Metre: Hendecasyllables
For most pupils the Catullus poems will be an entirely new experience; for teachers the challenge will be to allow the poems to speak for themselves and not to assume among pupils their own level of familiarity with the author's work. The three poems in *amor* represent three snapshots of Catullus' affair with Lesbia. For the latter see the *Cambridge Latin Course* Unit IVB, pp.109-11.
The discussion on this poem is a short synthesis of the sensitive and illuminating thoughts of R.O.A.M.Lyne, *Cambridge Latin Texts Series, Selections from Catullus* Poem 2, Handbook (CUP).

1 **bāsiātiōnēs:** this coinage from the colloquial *bāsium*, picked up by *bāsia* and *bāsiāre* in 9, has been made to look like the formal word *ōsculātiō* for humorous effect.

3 **quam magnus:** this and *quam multa* in 7, do not translate easily into English structure; suggest to pupils that the addition of 'which' helps - 'as many as the stars which…'.

4 **lāsarpīciferīs:** another coinage for similar reasons. Silphium (pupil's note) is asafoetida, a plant whose juice was used in cookery and medicine.

9 **tam tē bāsia multa bāsiāre:** 'that's how many kisses (it's enough for Catullus) to give you'.

10 **vēsānō:** comic exaggeration of the usual word *īnsānus*.

11-12 **quae…possint:** the relative clause is consecutive,'so many (kisses) that inquisitive people can…'.

Discussion

Teachers will decide for themselves how much background to introduce about Catullus but one important idea for pupils to grasp is that Lesbia is a *docta puella,* cultivated and sophisticated and well-educated; without this pupils will find the learned allusions puzzling. This in turn raises interesting (and not very easily answered) questions about girls' education versus boys'.

The opening of the poem presupposes a question from Lesbia, as if she has found Catullus' attention a little too much: 'just how many kisses *do* you want?' The fact that it is 'kissing' sets the light-hearted tone. And the answer to the implied question, 'Are you insatiable?' appears to be 'Yes!' The *doctus poēta* now has to persuade the *docta puella* in this mood into love. The notes above pick out humorous word-play which, together with the appeal to her *doctrīna* through the 'extravagantly learned section' (3-8) set out to make Lesbia smile at her own objections. The image of the sands is more than dry literary display: it is a parody for amusement, an exaggeration and Lesbia has the *doctrīna* to understand and the wit to see through it - for example the alliteration of *s* in 3-6 with its suggestions of desert-winds. The clichés here are given fresh life by the topographical and personal detail. With the image of the stars Catullus reaches the turning-point of the poem: their number is relevant because they see the secret loves of men, of Catullus and Lesbia. The poem is now personalised with the word *fūrtīvōs*, rich with associations of night, silence, privacy and illicit activities. As we re-enter the world of the lovers after the similes, the humorous tone resumes with *bāsia, bāsiāre* (9) and *vēsānō* (10) and the poem concludes with a comically applied superstition: knowing the precise number of something (here the kisses) gives malicious people power over others; but here they are frustrated because the kisses are too many to count.

Can she be faithful? (Catullus, Poem 109)

Metre: Elegiac couplets
There is a very full discussion of this poem in the Handbook to the first edition of the *Cambridge Latin Course* Unit IV, pp.94-7.

- **1-2** The first line can be read separately to make syntactical sense but it also, when we reach 2, forms part of a longer reported statement; the gloss in the pupil's text stresses the second idea.
  mea vīta: it may not be immediately obvious to pupils that this is the same girl as in the previous poem *quaeris, quot mihi bāsiātiōnēs*.
- **5 ut liceat nōbīs:** a result clause: 'so that we may...'.
- **6** The glosses given in the pupil's text are deliberately standard or

amor 25

neutral; in view of the discussion below teachers may like to investigate more subtle meanings for *sānctus, foedus* and *amīcitia*.

aeternum: the sense is predicative, 'extend this pact of ours (so that it is) lifelong'. It can be brought out in reading by emphasising *aeternum*.

Discussion

The poem falls into two separate parts: 1-2 with Lesbia's promise and 3-6 with Catullus' response, at the end of which the thoughts of the opening line reappear.

The first two lines strongly suggest that Catullus is addressing Lesbia face to face. *iūcundum* is emphatically placed and there is some doubt initially as to whether it is Lesbia's word or forms part of an interpretation of the *amōrem* by Catullus. By 3 we appreciate our misconception: 1-2 are an imaginary address to the girl and 3-6 a (real or imaginary) address to the gods, made clear by the change of person from *prōpōnis* to *possit* and *dīcat*. Clues to the poet's anxiety about the truthfulness of Lesbia's sentiments are then piled up: is she capable (*possit*) of promising truly, sincerely and from the heart? The implied answer is 'No'. The last two lines pick up and develop the religious language of *dī magnī, facite ut* (3). Clearly the poet thinks of a long relationship (*tōtā...vītā, aeternum*) based on trust and understanding (*foedus*), where a special relationship (*sānctae...amīcitiae*) depends on more than sexual attraction; one senses the strength of both his longing and his doubts.

Conflicting emotions (Catullus, Poem 85)

Metre: Elegiac couplet

A fuller discussion of this poem can be found in the Handbook to the first edition of the *Cambridge Latin Course* Unit IV, pp.88-90 and in the Handbook to Unit IVB, pp.76-7.

    1-2 faciam...fierī: amid other contrasts is the grammatical one of the active/passive relationship between *faciō/fīō*. Pupils need to have covered this if they are to pick up wider meanings in the poem.

Discussion
Lesbia is not mentioned but we can assume that she is at the centre of this very personal epigram. The key to the poem is the series of contrasts which pull Catullus in conflicting directions: 'he finds only confusion, contradiction and pain. He knows and yet he does not know what he feels for her.' There are contrasts of emotion (*ōdī, amō*), of person (*faciam, requīris*), of knowing rationally versus feeling emotionally (*nescio, sentiō*) and, leading out of the latter, the crucial one of doing and suffering (*faciam, fierī/ excrucior*).

The structure of the poem is special: each line opens with a statement followed by a comment on it; the identity of *requīris* is unclear - Catullus, Lesbia or the reader/listener? The dialogue form draws us into the dilemma; the ambiguous final and emphatic *excrucior* - is it love, hate or both? And all this in two lines.

Lesbia, it was suggested, is at the centre. Pupils may like to discuss how much the poem tells us about her and how much about Catullus.

Contradictions (Martial, *Epigrams* XII.47)

Metre: Elegiac couplet

It will be interesting to see how long it takes pupils unprompted to realise that this is not addressed to a woman. The first line does not carry a specific sexual reference but the second line uses vocabulary and expression firmly in the amatory mould. All the essential features of the epigram are here: the juxtaposition of idea and sound in line 1 and the careful arrangement of words in 2 around the central *possum vīvere,* pushing *nec tēcum* and *nec sine tē* to either end, with the punch right at the last. Pupils may enjoy exploring affinities with *ōdī et amō.*

Ovid picks a favourite at the races (Ovid, *Amores* III.2.1-14)

Metre: Elegiac couplets

These are the opening lines of a much longer poem; the rest could be read to pupils in translation and would be enjoyed. Teachers' likely familiarity with this section can lead them to forget that the Latin is conversational and

amor 27

difficult in places. The setting at the races will need preparation of words like *mēta, lōra, carcer, agitātor;* also pupils may not realise the relationship between Ovid, the girl and the charioteer. It would be useful to show Roger Dalladay's superb filmstrip *Circus Maximus;* there is a picture of a race-relief in the *Cambridge Latin Course* Unit IIIB, p.101.

1 **sedeō:** establish that Ovid is sitting next to a girl at the race-track watching the preliminaries to a day's racing. The race in 9-14 is hypothetical; the actual race comes later in the poem.

2 Chat-up lines have changed very little, it seems. *ille* refers to the charioteer.

3 **vēnī:** Ovid tells us in *Ars Amatoria* I.89-100 that the theatre was another excellent place to pick up girls (**ōtium** p.66). Note the chiastic word-order in this line: *loquerer tēcum…tēcum…sedērem.*

6 **quod iuvat:** 'what we (each) like'.

9 **sacrō dē carcere:** the description of the starting-gate as 'sacred' may rest upon the general religious associations of festivals. If there is a more specific reference, it could concern the god Consus who had a subterranean altar in the Circus, uncovered only on his festival days. Dalladay's filmstrip presents another possible explanation: the Piazza Armerina mosaic shows a scene outside the circus with three temples (portrayed above the *carcerēs*) at which charioteers have been praying; statues (of gods?) are shown on top of the *carcerēs.*

9-10 **hoc mihi contingat…insistam:** 'if I were this lucky…I will press on'. This type of mixed conditional sentence (present subjunctive…future indicative) is common in Ovid. The futures here seem truly 'vivid': Ovid is carried away as he fantasises. *mihi* contrasts with *illī* (8).

vehendus: in the sense of a present participle *passive* - 'being carried along'.

11-12 The techniques are: slackening the reins to let the horses go faster, lashing the horses and keeping as close as possible to the turning-posts to avoid losing ground.

Discussion

Would the attitudes of Ovid's audience to this poem differ from our own? Probably very little. A reading of the whole poem indicates a gentle if saucy humour and there is nothing to offend. Ovid seems to be intent on portraying himself to the girl, if not to the reader, as something of a love-sick youth (3-4 and 13-14) and the idea that he could slow down or stop in mid-race, on noticing the girl, is comic. The poem is particularly useful for our knowledge of how racing was organised. Pliny had different views on racing (*Letters* IX.6).

Ovid's ingenuity becomes evident if the pupils are asked to count up the number of ways in which the speaker exploits the Circus situation in order to chat the girl up. Of the hints and compliments in 2, 3-4, 5-6, 7-12, 13-14, only the flattery in 3-4 could be employed in other situations; the other chat-up lines are firmly tied to the Circus.

Pyrrha (Horace, *Odes* I.V)

Metre: Asclepiads

A Latin poem set out in formal stanzas may look unusual to pupils who have seen only hexameters or epigrams.

There are several difficult noun-adjective splits in this poem.

1 **gracilis:** the word is used to refer to a young adolescent (*puer*).
   rosā: singular for plural, as *multā* shows. The perfume that often accompanies an erotic scene (ancient or modern) is here supplied by the rose-petals sprinkled around.
   Note the brilliant arrangement of words in 1 which reflects the actual situation: *tē* (Pyrrha) in the embrace of the *gracilis puer*, both of them surrounded by roses, *multā...in rosā*.

2 **perfūsus:** this refers to the boy's oiling and perfuming (*liquidīs... odōribus*) of his hair.

3 **Pyrrha:** the Greek name suggests auburn or red-gold hair and is picked up by *flāvam...comam* (4); *flāvus* is a honey-gold colour. She is obviously a courtesan.
   antrō: almost certainly an artificial garden feature.

4 **religās:** the hair is tied for simplicity, not elaborately set.

amor 29

5 **simplex munditiīs:** traditionally translated 'simple in your elegance' but untranslatable. Both words refer to her simple and tasteful attractiveness and are not really an oxymoron.

fidem (mūtātam): 'altered (or capricious) fidelity'.

6-7 **aspera...ventīs:** the phrase suggests a calm situation suddenly becoming turbulent. The metaphor of the sea is found again in *nescius aurae fallācis* (11-12) where the boy does not understand Pyrrha's fickle favour; the metaphor extends all through the fourth stanza. There are weather metaphors in modern love-songs.

8 **īnsolēns:** the boy has had no experience of women. *ēmīrābitur* prepares for the idea; the word occurs only here in classical literature and Horace has almost certainly coined it for this place. The sense is, 'will show utter amazement': the boy's complete astonishment at finding that love isn't all roses is a comment not only on this but on all love-affairs of this kind.

9 **tē...aureā:** perhaps a reference to her hair, more likely a reference to the brief golden moments of love; *crēdulus* is then neatly juxtaposed with *aureā* - the inexperienced, gullible youth contrasted with the dazzling, experienced Pyrrha. The two words have almost a syntactical relationship: he believes that she will always be like this.

10 **vacuam:** 'unattached' or 'available' for only a while as *nescius aurae fallācis* makes clear.

13 **intemptāta nitēs:** both words can be used of both the sea and the girl.

13-16 It was common practice to hang on a temple wall a (bronze) tablet to acknowledge an escape from danger; pictures were sometimes used to make the message clearer. The tablet was often put up to fulfil a vow (*vōtum*). Where sailors were involved their actual clothes (and tackle) could be dedicated - as Horace invites us to imagine here. Pupils may have seen votive tablets in Catholic churches on the Continent.

15-16 **potentī...maris deō:** 'to the god who has power over the sea'.

Discussion

The questions, 'Who was Pyrrha?' 'Which *puer* did Horace have in mind?' 'Where was the grotto?' can be answered conclusively only by reference to the many literary conventions which will be rightly regarded as beyond most pupils at this stage. Pupils could profitably be guided towards the view that the poem loses very little if such questions lack biographical or geographical answers; rather it is the type of situation and Horace's attitude to it that are under examination.

The starting-point here can be Pyrrha and the significance of her name (see above); the discussion then leads on to *flāvam, simplex munditiīs, aureā, intemptāta nitēs* and the metaphorical allusions in *aspera...aequora, aurae fallācis*. The *puer* is characterised as young (*gracilis...puer*), eager to impress (*perfūsus liquidīs...odōribus*) and inexperienced (*īnsolēns, crēdulus*); more obliquely too he fails to understand risks in love (*heu quotiēns...flēbit*) and has naïve hopes (*spērat*). If one sets the pictures of the boy and girl together one sees the way in which a Pyrrha's innocence in appearance is not a good guide to her behaviour, the crucial fact that the *gracilis puer* fails to see. With a very able group, discussion could lead on to how Horace injects fresh ideas into literary conventions such as the farewell to love and the treacherous girl. An important point is that the first experiences of love in the life of most Roman boys would have been basically commercial; sooner or later the ingenuous youth comes up against this fact and the shock is always a total surprise. Horace, who has seen it all before, manages to add a new twist to the theme; the poem turns on the contrast between the neophyte and the hardened Horace. Some of these ideas are difficult to get across to pupils as modern analogies in British society of the present day do not readily present themselves.

The metaphor of the sea is a powerful theme and serves to bind the poem; it allows Horace to claim he has retired from such amorous adventures.

Teachers could invite pupils to experiment with reading the poem aloud: should the tone be indignant and aggressive or detached, indulgent and amused? From this approach or from others will arise the question of whether in the fourth stanza Horace presents himself as one of Pyrrha's former victims.

Alcyone fears for her husband Ceyx who has to go on a journey (Ovid, Metamorphoses XI.415-29, 439-43)

Metre: Hexameters

This passage is an extract from early in a long episode: Ceyx is to travel to consult an oracle of Apollo and his wife is struck with foreboding (this passage); Ceyx is drowned in a storm at sea; in a dream Alcyone learns of the disaster and next day finds her husband's body on the sea shore (Penguin, pp.257-65).

1 **cōnsiliī:** Ceyx's intention to travel to consult an oracle is not obvious from the passage and requires explanation. It leads into the idea of his breaking the news to his wife.

2 **Alcyonē:** the name is used twice, here by Ovid as an apostrophe and in 9 by Alcyone of herself. Together with *tē* (2) and *fidissima* (1) it serves to personalise the crisis, to strengthen her appeal and help us to appreciate their mutual love. Pupils will need help with the unfamiliar idea of apostrophe which will be disconcerting so early in this piece in 1; establish that it is Ovid addressing Alcyone.

4 **obīt:** perfect tense, contracted form of *obiit*.

6 The sobbing sound of *singultū* is noteworthy and combines with the pauses on the double consonants (*-rr-* and *-ll-*) in *interrumpente* and *querellās* to give an effective line after the stock ideas in 2-5.

17-18 As her speech ends Alcyone gasps out the words with *patiar, pariterque, pariter.* Ovid, with an eye to verbal tricks, suggests togetherness with similar-sounding line-endings: *ferēmus* and *ferēmur*. Note also the use of *ferō* in two different senses; one can bring out the pun by using the translation 'bear'.

Discussion

Some pupils are bound to see Alcyone's reaction as hysterical: a modern counterpart, faced with a business trip by her husband, would hardly behave so, even if it did involve a cross-channel ferry. The key will be to guide pupils to an appreciation of the ancients' view of travel, particularly by sea: it was undertaken by few and usually only when necessary, was fraught with danger and, if there was a disaster at sea, could involve loss of burial which meant distress for the souls of the dead.

There are both drama and pathos in the passage. Alcyone's address starts in standard fashion with rhetorical questions; she uses ideas familiar to the poetry of departing lovers - she blames herself first (7) and asks how he can love her and yet leave her (8-9), finishing with the tormented thought that he loves her more when he is away (10). The visions of 12-13 - real or imaginary - would be far more compelling to ancient peoples than to us. Appeal takes over from reproach at 14 and pathos enters as she begs to be taken with him.

Not of course a love-poem as such, the passage has several echoes of love-poetry, especially elegy (the separation of lovers, tears, pallor, blame, reproach). In such a short passage it will be hard for pupils to see what is clear from the whole episode: Ceyx and Alcyone, who are so devoted, are at the mercy of the power of nature - notice the passives *iactābimur* (16) and *ferēmur* (18).

This passage was included as an example of married love and teachers might ask pupils if it carries conviction. One approach is to look for the words in 16-18 which emphasise 'togetherness'; pupils may grasp Ovid's main point if they are asked why Alcyone wants to take part in a journey that may mean death for her.

Love will not let the poet sleep (Petronius fragment)

Metre: Elegiac couplets

The author of the *Satyrica* was probably the Petronius who was a courtier of Nero. Even more uncertainty surrounds the authorship of the thirty or so short poems traditionally attributed to him; but their spirit is clearly different from that of the major work.

- 1 **compositus:** the verb is used here of getting oneself comfortable in bed.
- 2 **somnō lūmina victa dabam:** 'my eyes were overcome with tiredness and I was falling asleep'.
- 3, 14 **Amor, Cupīdo:** essentially the same and representing here the desire of man for woman.

amor 33

5 **famulus:** more of a personal slave, an attendant.
6 The commas here will puzzle pupils; the *iō* and *dūre* need isolating.
7 **pedibus nūdīs tunicāque solūtā:** this possibly refers simply to a hasty exit from bed and home or there could be traces of magical ideas, seen in elegiacs elsewhere: bare feet touching the ground assisted the process of magic, whereas any knots in clothing impeded it.
8 **impediō... expediō:** the sense is quite literal: the poet is all over the place but getting nowhere. This epigrammatic expression is then clarified and expanded in the next couplet (9-10). Note the rhyme, repetition and identical half-line rhythms which help the sense of starting and stopping. The two elisions make for speed.
9-10 The alliteration, especially of *p*, again heightens the emphasis of starting and stopping.

Discussion

This poem has much in common with the elegies of Propertius and Tibullus; its playful tone is established firmly, however, in 3-6. The familiar picture of the lover alone opens the poem; is he simply sleepy or is there a reason for his being tired? Is it that he has been too sexually active? Amid the humour of 3-6 begins the idea of man as a slave to Love and by implication to woman: Love is unrelenting (*saevus*) and he who disobeys is *dūrus*. The lover obeys but he dithers and keeps changing his mind - perhaps he cannot decide which girl to choose (*mīlle puellās* 5) or perhaps there is a conflict between desire and propriety (*pudor* 10). The poem concludes with the lover's fear that Cupido will not let him rest in bed, but whose is the command (*imperium*)? Love's or the poet's own? There is a nightmarish, feverish, driven quality about this piece; the poet cannot escape the demands of sex.

Discussion could centre on how love is portrayed in this piece. One starting-point would be to ask why the poet feels *pavor* (cf.13) at the thought of sleep and bed.

ōtium

The good life (Martial, Epigrams V.20)

Metre: Hendecasyllables

1 **Mārtiālis:** this is Iulius Martialis, the poet's closest friend and perhaps patron; he was wealthy and cultivated.

2,7,10 **liceat...nōssēmus...essent:** the sequence of tenses in the condition is not what one would expect but the sense 'if we were allowed...we would (not) know...these would be the places' seems clear.

nōssēmus = nōvissēmus: 'we would have learnt' and so 'we would know', 'we would be familiar with'. The contracted form plus tense shift in English will be difficult for pupils. The negative idea in *nec* could be rendered by 'we would know nothing of'.

5 Martial is thinking of clients dancing attendance on patrons, especially at the morning *salūtātiō*.

6 The forum was the home of the Basilica Julia, the law-court associated with disputes about inheritances; it was also the setting for funeral speeches as well as financial deals.

7 **imāginēs superbās:** the impressive-looking funeral busts of ancestors of the wealthy, kept in the atrium and paraded on the anniversary of the death of the deceased.

8 **gestātio:** this seems to suggest some sort of ride - on a horse or in a *sella gestātōria*.

9 The Aqua Virgo was known for the refreshing coldness of its water.

10 The sense requires *(nostra) loca...(nostrī) labōrēs* 'our haunts...our interests'.

13 **nōbīs pereunt et imputantur:** the image here is of Fate keeping a tally and charging to man's account every day that passes - and then it's gone *(pereunt)*. This may have been seen on sundials.

14 **quisquam:** the word, as usual, anticipates a negative response; here the thought is 'No (but we still don't know how to live)'.

Discussion

This is the traditional cry for more time to do the things one wants to do rather than those one has to do. Many of the ideas will be familiar from the *Cambridge Latin Course* but pupils may be interested to hear read similar thoughts from the contemporary Pliny, I.9. The tone is established in a monologue-dialogue frame where the poet is not so much addressing his friend but a vision of their friendship and life; the usual images are set side by side and there are few surprises in the lists. The most original ideas come in the twist in 11-14: Martial proposes that one should put *bonōs sōlēs* to better use by indulging oneself.

Epigram X.47 (**dē cultū deōrum et vītā hominum**, p.88) makes an interesting comparison.

Pupils might be asked how the two lists differ. If they can offer only 'unpleasant and pleasant activities' they should be prompted to look for more precise contrasts, e.g. public/private, pleasing others/pleasing oneself.

The pleasures of country life (Horace, *Epodes* II.1-8,23-8)

Metre: Iambic trimeters and dimeters alternating
The passage is an extract from a much longer poem.

1. **negōtiīs:** the word refers to money-matters which do not concern the farmer; such worries deny a man peace and leisure (*neg-ōtium*) and smack of the city. Business is thus seen as the aberration from the ideal of *ōtium*.

3-4 The farmer has inherited his lands and cattle and thus pays no rent; he has no need to borrow money at interest.

5. **mīles:** '(as) a soldier, (he)...'. Pupils may need help with *mīles* in apposition to the unexpressed pronoun.

5-6 The reference is to the days before the professional army when the farmer responded to the war-cry, put down his farming tools, picked up a sword and went to fight as a soldier. The farmer has not been tempted to brave the sea as a merchant either.

7-8 The forum is associated with vexatious law-suits; the houses of the powerful imply being obligated to a powerful citizen.

10 **tenācī:** the pupils' gloss 'firm' implies a deep, lush grass that you can settle into comfortably.
11 **altīs...rīpīs:** in summer, when the water-level is low, the banks look much taller.
14 **quod invītet:** 'to invite' (purpose clause, which personifies the water). *quod* refers back to the water's gentle sound.

Discussion

The peace and calm of the countryside are the subject of this passage; pupils may be reminded of the *Cambridge Latin Course* Unit IVA, Stage 35. Comparison and further reading could include Tibullus I.1 and Virgil, *Georgics* II.458-540. The list of those pursuits followed and those rejected is standard: they appear in so far as they promote or preclude peace of mind. The commonplaces of this idealised countryside could be used to prompt pupils to suggest modern idealised examples - roses around the country cottage door, etc. Pupils will need to realise that ideas such as those in 2 depend upon the view that there was once a Golden Age when all was peaceful and well.

Poetry and friendship (Catullus, Poem 50)

Metre: Hendecasyllables

Catching the right tone in English for Catullus' vocabulary is difficult and this poem presents many challenges; pupils can usefully be asked to suggest alternatives for the glosses in their text once the basic sense is established.

1 **Licinī:** C.Licinius Calvus Macer was a talented orator as well as a poet. He was the subject of several poems of Catullus, 14, 53 and 96, of which 14 would be of interest in translation for ideas on the *novī poētae*.
2 **tabellīs:** waxed wooden writing-tablets with raised wooden frames, tied with leather straps at one side, no more than perhaps five together and used for non-permanent forms of writing. There is a picture in the *Cambridge Latin Course,* Unit I, Stage 10.

5 **numerō...hōc...illōc:** a variety of lyric metres were used in the *versiculī* (4).

7-13 Catullus uses the language of love-poetry to express how deeply he has been affected: *incēnsus* (8), *miserum* (9) and *furōre* (11). Interspersed are words which have special significance for Catullus' circle: *lepōre* (7), *facētiīs* (8) and the diminutive *ocellōs* (10). Taken together the vocabulary may suggest a strong attraction for Licinius; however, the intense feeling could equally be attributed to the excitement of indulging one's enthusiasm in the company of a kindred spirit.

If one wants to press the point, the vocabulary *cibus* (9), *somnus* (10) and *lūcem* (12) suggest that the meeting with Licinius was the afternoon before and that we have travelled with Catullus overnight to the next day, the occasion of writing the poem.

18 **precēs...nostrās:** this is the request alluded to in 13.

19 **dēspuās:** this strong word may confirm the inference that Catullus would welcome more than ordinary friendship and fears that Licinius may reject it. It could simply be humorous exaggeration, as the following lines suggest. Pupils will find 18 and 19 easier to understand if *ōrāmus* and *ocelle* are isolated.

ocelle: this metaphorical use will need distinguishing from the literal meaning in 10; the sense is 'my dear friend', 'apple of my eye'.

20 The invocation of the goddess of retribution is light-hearted; the idea is that she will punish Licinius if he refuses Catullus' *precēs*.

21 **cavētō:** the unfamiliar formal imperative is used here with the infinitive as an alternative for *cave (nē) laedās*, the construction seen in 18 and 19. The rather grand-sounding word ends the poem with a mock-solemn threat.

Discussion

One suspects that perseverance will be needed over the central idea here; pupils may not readily respond to the image of two young men entertaining each other by writing light verse as a leisure pursuit. Pupils could be asked how succeeding generations may view their own activities: making music in rock-bands in small groups is hardly as different as they may imagine.

38 Commentary: verse selections

Time considerations will restrict how far one can go into the activities of Catullus' circle of fellow poets, their views and their philosophies. The essential features here are that an afternoon writing verse in the company of a sophisticated friend has left Catullus excited and unable to sleep and requesting another meeting. Pupils will need to consider that the opening six lines are background for the reader; Licinius obviously knew this already. It will be interesting to see whether they pick up any homosexual overtones; discussion could centre on 11ff. where the erotic character of the vocabulary perhaps suggests they were writing light-hearted love epigrams to each other. Only on returning home does Catullus realise he has fallen in love.

There is a wealth of opportunity here to compare and contrast ancient and modern ideas of leisure. These two men were clever, cultured and well-off; how did others entertain themselves? The Anna Perenna piece in this section talks of the *plēbs* but it concerns a large group on only one day. And in modern times? A drink in a bar, a meal, a game of squash, a video - the list is long. Will any pupils have experienced the same *intellectual* excitement and rapport that possessed Catullus? Pupils may like to consider whether *reddēns mūtua* (6) implies a competitive element. Were the verses essentially repartee? Could pupils write some of their own? Limericks provide a familiar starting-point.

Catullus invites a friend to dinner (Catullus, Poem 13)

Metre: Hendecasyllables

There is an interesting pair of translations of this poem in *Aestimanda*, 49-50 (Balme and Warman, OUP).

    2 **sī tibi dī favent:** the sense is quite casual and to be taken with *paucīs diēbus* - 'if you're lucky' or 'God willing'.

    5 **sale:** a pun on the two meanings is intended: after *vīnō* we expect *sale* to mean 'salt' but by the end of the line the sense of 'wit' is appreciated.

    6 **venuste:** an important word used by Catullus of his friends, it denotes those who have charm and discrimination. The link with Venus will need pointing out; it is significant.

8 The poverty of the poet is proverbial.
12 **Venerēs Cupīdinēsque:** 'all the powers of Charm and Desire there are' (C.J.Fordyce, *Catullus,* OUP). Pupils could compare this translation with the one offered in their text and suggest others.

Discussion
Catullus has taken a conventional type of occasional verse - the invitation to a meal - and added some original features of his own, which is where pupils' interest may usefully be focused. Biographical details of Fabullus will probably only obscure discussion but one may like to ask whether it matters more who the recipient is than the *sort* of person he is (*viz. venuste* 6) and also whether the dinner is ever seriously intended to happen.

It was conventional to be asked to take a gift to a Roman dinner party and lines 1-5 explore this theme: the suspected light humour of line 2 with its original touch of procrastination is confirmed by *sale* and *omnibus cachinnīs* in 5; Catullus seems too poor to provide anything for the dinner. With *venuste* we sense that the poem turns on the appreciation of those with sensibilities: Fabullus will receive 'undiluted affection' and the poet can quote nothing finer than that - or can he? Here comes what R.O.A.M.Lyne calls the 'calculated humorous surprise' (*Cambridge Latin Texts Series, Catullus Handbook,* p.41): a special scent, associated with love and involving Lesbia (*meae puellae*), will be Catullus' second contribution. The careful word order of 14 with *nāsum* delayed emphasises the power of it: it is a gift from the gods and powers of Love to Lesbia, and Fabullus will be given some (evidently the use of perfume generally was common at Roman dinner-parties). Fabullus, as *venustus,* will appreciate that Catullus' contribution of true friendship and of perfume, an aphrodisiac with all its amusement potential, is not so insignificant after all. Some scholars take the view that the extravagant promise of *merōs amorēs* 'the quintessence of love' cannot be adequately fulfilled unless Lesbia herself accompanies the perfume. In her divine fragrance she embodies the perfume.

A good place to find a girl (Ovid, *Ars Amatoria* I.89-100)

Metre: Elegiac couplets

Pupils should be told that this is an extract from a much longer work. A little earlier in Book I, Ovid announces that his advice to the lover will be three-fold: finding a girl (our passage is from that section), winning over the girl and making the love last. The *Ars Amatoria* was the *carmen* Ovid refers to when he reflects on the cause of his exile (*Tristia* II.207): *perdiderint cum mē duo crīmina, carmen et error.*

1 **tū:** much of the work is naturally in the second person.

   vēnāre: the imperative form of a deponent verb may well be unfamiliar.

2 **vōtō fertiliōra tuō:** 'even more productive than you could wish for'.

3-4 The sense of *quod* + subjunctive is 'someone for you to...'. Note the elaborate word-patterning of the chiasmus: a girl you would want to love and keep (*amēs* and *tenēre velīs*) as against a girl you would deceive and give up (*lūdere* and *semel tangās*), where *semel tangās* suggests a one-off relationship.

5 **redit itque:** 'goes back and forward', the sound assisting the idea of repeated action. The reversal of the natural order is for metrical convenience.

5-9 As usual with similes the picking out of the correspondences will be fruitful. The scene suggested is that of women busily filing into the theatre in an unbroken line, perhaps bringing their picnic with them, followed by that of the women inside the theatre as a natural haunt (*saltūsque suōs*) turning their attention from one attraction to another. *cultissima* strongly suggests dressing for the occasion and being on the look-out for a pick-up.

10 Ovid interjects his own experience, partly to remind us that he is controlling the narrative, partly to keep the light-hearted tone going: Ovid has himself been spoilt for choice.

11 An opportunity to introduce pupils to a simple example of chiasmus and to Ovid's verbal skill generally. They could try to reproduce the chiastic effect in English, either in a translation of this line ('to watch they come, come to be watched themselves') or in an example of their own ('they acquitted Smith but Jones was sent to prison'). A literary example: 'For we that live to please, must please to live'

(Dr Johnson, *The Vanity of Human Wishes*).

spectātum: supine of purpose with *veniunt*: the women come to watch - both the show *and* the men.

12 'that place involves the loss of one's chastity'.

Discussion

If a charge of sexism is levelled at Ovid by pupils, one may like to consider whether, given the conditions and respective positions of men and women, the ancient world could produce anything else. Could one ever read in Latin a poem by a woman about women going to the theatre to pick up men? And yet no one should suppose it somehow did not happen; the poem itself suggests as much - the simile in 7-8, the *cultissima fēmina* of 9 and the obvious line 11. There is the assumption in Ovid (and perhaps still today?) that both sexes are interested in a pick-up but that the initiative lies with the man. Pupils may enjoy discussing whether modern attitudes are very different and which social occasions Ovid would choose today - it is unlikely that the theatre will be one. The tricky question of the social standing of the women involved in Roman times needs to be considered, too; simple modern analogies can be misleading.

It is an accident of the selection that this particular passage gives few clues about who is chasing whom in the opening lines: is the *tū* male or female? Apart from the English title the sense becomes clear only in 9 (*fēmina*) and 11 (*ipsae*). It will be interesting to see if pupils spot this but they should be told that in the wider poem the sense is quite explicit.

How ordinary people enjoy a festival (Ovid, *Fasti* III.523-40)

Metre: Elegiac couplets

Pupils may like to know that this is not an individual poem but a passage from the *Fasti*, Ovid's account in verse of the religious observances of the Roman calendar; he had reached June when he was banished in AD 8 and the work is unfinished. Although this passage contains many humorous touches, Ovid's purpose in writing the *Fasti* was a serious one. He was conscious that the observances he was describing were very ancient and provided important evidence for the venerability of Rome and her history.

There is a good deal of unfamiliar vocabulary here; the lines would benefit from preliminary work such as reading out loud and comprehension questions to establish early the images of camping out, drinking and singing and dancing.

- **1 fēstum geniāle:** the festival was evidently celebrated just out of Rome to the north in an orchard dedicated to Anna Perenna. As her name suggests, she seems to have been associated with the ending of one year and the beginning of the next. March was the first month of the old Roman calendar and a feast was held on the Ides, to mark what was the first full moon of the new year. *geniāle* establishes the happy, sexually active atmosphere of this event.
- **2 advena:** the Tiber is foreign in the sense that it has flowed through Etruscan regions before reaching Rome; this apostrophe, rather high-flown, is presumably light-hearted.
  Thybri: Greek vocative.
- **3 plēbs:** the implication is that this is a festival popular especially with the ordinary people of the city who come out to have a good time. At several points in the passage one senses these are young people (4,9,16); the atmosphere is suggestive of bank holidays, rock festivals and the secular aspects of Christmas.
- **4 accumbit...suā:** the phrase is suggestive of love-making.
- **6 quibus:** the so-called dative of agent, popular with Ovid.
- **6-8 facta...est, imposuēre:** as a present tense sense is needed, translate, 'some have been known to...'.
  statuēre: in a subordinate clause, can bear a past sense.
- **8** Pupils need to realise that togas used a large amount of cloth: the straight edge of this semicircular garment was about 5.5 metres; the width 2.25 metres.
- **9 calent:** suggestive of passion, too.
- **9-12** This is clearly some sort of drinking game by numbers perhaps linked with prayers for long life; the introduction of such as Nestor and Sibyl proves just how determined they were to drink themselves silly: cf. *titubant* (17). The 'drinking the years' suggests the very nature of Anna Perenna as a goddess. 70 years would require about 3.5 litres of drink.

ōtium 43

10 **sūmant:** subjunctive in virtual *oratio obliqua*.
12 **Sibylla:** a prophetess, inspired (usually) by Apollo. Of the various Sibyls around the Mediterranean, the Sibyl at Cumae was the best known. When asked by Apollo, who loved her, to choose a gift she asked to live as many years as grains of sand in her hand but forgot to ask for youth. Her aged and decrepit body became legendary.
13-15 With all the drinking there should be no surprise at the robust antics here. Ovid piles up the activities with *et cantant...et iactant...et dūcunt*. Notice the *dūc...dū...c...c...* alliteration in 15, reinforcing the picture of unsophisticated cavortings.
14 Ancient dancing made much use of hands and arms. *manūs* here must mean 'arms'.
15 **positō...cratēre:** this suggests that the bowl is placed on the ground and danced around.
16 **amīca:** suggestive of a courtesan entertaining.
17 **cum redeunt, titubant:** the dactyls suggest their less than secure progress.
sunt spectācula vulgī: 'they are a public spectacle'.
18 **fortūnātōs:** the word is often used in exclamations to describe those particularly well treated by fate or divinity, here Anna Perenna; the crowd may well have shouted out the word - the heavy syllables suggest so.

Discussion

There is no obscure imagery for pupils to grasp and a careful reading will form the basis of a discussion of holidays for religious festivals and celebrations; comparison with those of today is an attractive possibility. Some thought may be given to Ovid's attitude to the jollifications: is he being critical of their coarse enjoyment in lines 13-16? The successive *cantant, iactant, dūcunt*; the contemptuous *quidquid didicēre theātrīs*; the use of *facilēs* with *manūs* and *dūrās* with *choreās*; and the picture of the hussy all serve to suggest so. Which people would criticise today's secularisation of Christmas celebrations? Can we dictate how people should spend their leisure? How much is leisure bound up with religious festivals in the ancient and modern worlds?

vīta rūstica et vīta urbāna

The city, hour by hour (Martial, *Epigrams* IV.8)

The chief interest in this epigram for pupils will probably be the light it throws on the daily round in the city of Rome; for Martial, however, its chief thrust lies in engineering a compliment to Domitian, under a light-hearted request to Euphemus to show the Emperor his poems.

Metre: Elegiac couplets

1 **prīma...hōra:** the timing of the hours of the Roman day depended of course on the season and the amount of daylight available: sunrise (when the first hour began) was some three hours earlier in midsummer than in midwinter (and sunset was accordingly later or earlier); daylight hours in midsummer were about 1 hour 15 minutes long, in midwinter about 45 minutes. Without the accurate time-pieces which we rely upon, the Romans must have had a much less precise attitude to the passing of the hours than we have; candles, sun-dials and water-clocks cannot possibly have been used by the majority to gauge the passing of time with precision.

salūtantēs: a reference to the *salūtātiō* when the *cliēns* goes to greet the *patrōnus* at his home. Martial is not keen on the practice, as is suggested here by *conterit*.

Lines 1-2 have a harsh alliterative effect; note the repetition of *t* and *c*.

2 **raucōs:** this is proleptic, '...and makes them hoarse'. The courts sat early.

Martial omits mention of the fourth hour; the words of the text suggest that the period from the third to the fifth hours was spent in continuous activity.

4 **quiēs:** with the main part of the working day over, the sixth hour sees a siesta and no one works after the seventh. The sound of the line (especially the repetition of *s*) reflects the greater sense of peace.

5 After the working day, a visit to the palaestra was followed by one to the baths. *nitidīs* refers to the oil (mixed with wax and earth according to Juvenal) which wrestlers rubbed on their bodies.

6 **nōna:** the hour of the *cēna*.
7 **decima:** the meal itself is over and the drinking has begun; this marks the change in direction in the poem towards Martial's own interest. Softer sounds (*l, m, -or*) reflect peace again.
8, 9 **ambrosiās...nectare:** ambrosia and nectar were the traditional food and drink of the gods.
10 **pōcula parca:** Suetonius (*Domitian* 21) tells us that Domitian drank little.
11 **iocōs:** these are the epigrams in the *libellī* (7).

Discussion

This catalogue of the ceaseless round of city tasks provides a contrast with other poems in the section which stress the freedom and peace of the countryside. Teachers may like to refer in translation to other examples of similar themes: Juvenal I.127-34; Horace, *Satires* II.6 (the beginning); Pliny I.9. Notice how Martial enhances the predictable and repetitive nature of the activities by using end-stopped lines in 1-6; only with 7 and the change of direction does the sense run over the end of the line.

Martial uses several pieces of vocabulary to compliment Domitian and imply his divinity: *ambrosiās, bonus, aetheriō...nectare, ingentī...manū*. Any reference to Jupiter (*bonus* and *aetherius* are commonly used of him) is characteristically held back till the last word of the epigram. The sense of the last line and a half is that Martial wants Domitian to hear his poems when he is relaxed and in a good mood; just as Thalia would not attempt to secure a favour from Jupiter at a badly chosen moment, so there is a right time and a wrong time for Domitian, Jupiter's counterpart on earth, to hear cheeky verse. Martial here presents a full-blown deification of the *reigning* emperor.

Pupils familiar with Martial's epigrams will want to know where the joke is and there could be a useful discussion on the nature of the genre. If they are asked, 'Would the poem have been better if it had begun at 7?' they may notice the mild surprise effect of the change of direction within the epigram (1-6 being almost a red herring) and perhaps appreciate the 'snapshots' of Roman life in the first half of the poem.

The sights, sounds and seasons of the countryside (Ovid, *Remedia Amoris* 175-84, 187-90)

The passage is from Ovid's work *Remedia Amoris,* advice to a young man on how to fall *out* of love. The first suggestion - avoiding having too much spare time - is followed by a list of diversions the countryside can offer to the love-sick.

Metre: Elegiac couplets

- **1ff.** The significance of the repeated *aspice* with *ecce* is taken up in the Discussion; Ovid is addressing a young man in love; the imperatives in 1-5 are addressed to him.
- **7** Pan-pipes will be familiar to pupils, the pitch of the notes depending on the length of the reed; several reeds were tied in a row to allow a scale to be played when blown into.

Discussion

Pupils clearly will not know the wider context and thus it will be difficult to establish the light-hearted tone of this short piece. The repeated *aspice* with *ecce* suggest such a tone - a whistle-stop guided tour of the chief sights; from here pupils could be invited to say whether any of Ovid's pictures of the country come as a surprise or seem traditional. The view arrived at will probably be that the images are too neatly packaged to be original (pupils can compare *ō fōns Bandusiae* in this section): the apples weighing down the branches, the river, the sheep, the goats, the shepherd - one could perhaps stop reading around line 5 and ask pupils what else they *think* Ovid will go on to describe. Lines 11-12 confirm the suspicion: two lines, each split in half, each half giving us a commonplace of a season; indeed, one could repeat the question half-way through 12 by which time everyone should be able to predict the subject matter of what is coming next and even perhaps some of the detail. The lines suggest too a familiar art-form, quadripartite mosaics of the four seasons: in his brief description Ovid is assuming a familiarity with these on the part of the reader. Teachers may spot several echoes of Virgil; they may suspect a little pastiche is not far away. Ovid's consciousness of the pastoral convention and his flippant attitude to it are especially evident in 8 *nec dēsunt*: 'the obligatory dogs are, of course, included in my description'.

The poem is a rose-tinted view of the country, over-romanticised and seen from a town-dweller's viewpoint; notice the use of *rūsticus* (13), a word implying tone and colour and the opposite of *urbānus*. (The town and country mouse poem in this section could be used to make this clear. See especially the comment on 2-3, p.51.) Pupils could be asked to suggest examples of modern stereotyped life-styles - idyllic country cottages, glamorous city jobs, idealised family life in television advertisements.

Thoughts of home (Ovid, *Ex Ponto* I.VIII.29-38)

The poem is written from exile at Tomis (modern Constanza), on the shores of the Black Sea, in the form of a letter to his friend Severus (*tū* 1); Ovid has begun by complaining of his hardship generally and has moved on specifically to lament that he even has to fight to ward off the locals, the Getae. It is in this context that he reminisces about his friends, his family and the sights of the city of Rome.

Metre: Elegiac couplets

  1 **nec tū crēdiderīs:** a variant of *nē* with perfect subjective to express a negative command, often a forceful one.

  5ff. Pupils may need to be guided to an appreciation that Ovid is seeing the sights in his mind's eye; *reminīscor* (3) and *subit* (4, 8) will help as well as the more difficult language of 6.

  7-8 **fora:** Augustus added the Forum Augusti to the Forum Romanum and Forum Caesaris to cope with increasing imperial business.

  aedēs: according to the *Res Gestae*, 20, Augustus restored 82 temples.

  theātra: *Res Gestae*, 20 and 21 tells us that Augustus restored the Theatre of Pompey and built the Theatre of Marcellus. The phrase *marmore tēcta* recalls Augustus' boast according to Suetonius that he had found the city built of brick and left it built of marble (Suetonius, *Augustus* 28).

  porticus: colonnades were often found as adjuncts to fora, temples and theatres; they were designed to stroll or take exercise in.

aequātā...humō: this refers to earth-works often necessary as a preliminary to building.

10 **stāgna, eurīpī:** these were probably both features of the Gardens of Agrippa, in the Campus Martius.

Virgineus...liquor: the Aqua Virgo supplied the Baths of Agrippa, the first public set in Rome.

Discussion

Pupils may possibly know something of Ovid's exile and, in any case, the title, *Thoughts of home,* will suggest his being away from home. However, it will be interesting to see if pupils make the connection directly between the poem and his exile (AD 8); this extract from a longer piece hardly makes it obvious. Ovid himself refers to two reasons for the exile - *carmen et error,* the first undoubtedly the *Ars Amatoria,* the second unclear (*Tristia* II.207).

It is in this context that we should view the poet's longing for Rome; the sense of the first line is that Ovid initially will not ask for a return to Rome (the *whole* poem makes it clear that he is asking to be relocated in a less oppressive place than Tomis) but then the longing for Rome breaks through in 2. Here the line is carefully structured around the diaeresis: the second half of the line contains his true position; *tamen* makes this clear. We share with the poet the fresh significance not only of family and friends but also of those features of urban life which one normally takes for granted and are missed only when one is not able to enjoy them. Pupils could be invited to suggest what they would have written of their own home town. The poem is more than a list, however: Ovid strikes a plangent note with *dulcēs amīcī* (3), *cārā coniuge* and *nāta* (4) and the bleakly honest *quaerit et illa tamen* (2).

Astute pupils may see in the eulogy of the public buildings a veiled compliment to Augustus, responsible for so many of them - and for Ovid's exile. They will be interested to know that the flattery did not succeed in gaining Ovid a reprieve.

A country spring (Horace, Odes III.13)

It is important to draw pupils' attention to the vocabulary page of their text where a good deal of help is given with word-order in this poem.

Metre: Asclepiads

1 **ō:** stress that this word carries in Latin much more intensity of (especially religious) feeling than it can in modern English where it sounds archaic when used with a vocative; it is appreciated perhaps only in hymns nowadays ('O God, our help in ages past').
Bandusiae: perhaps a spring on Horace's farm but otherwise unknown.

2 Wine and flowers were used at most religious ceremonies. Pupils may like to know of the Roman festival of Fontinalia for springs and wells on October 13th and compare with well-dressing in Derbyshire.

5 **et venerem et proelia:** 'the battles of love' - a hendiadys.

6-7 **gelidōs...rubrō:** as often in Horace each adjective implies the contrary of the other: warm blood and clear water (as well as the obvious cold water and red blood).

9 **Canīculae:** the Dog Star is in conjunction with the sun in July and is associated with hot weather (cf. dog days).

13 Pupils may be unaware that the names of famous springs are common in classical literature (e.g. Egeria, near Rome - now the name of an Italian mineral water).

14 **mē dīcente:** causal sense.

14-16 The picture is of a hollowed-out rocky cliff, shaded by an evergreen tree, probably on a hill-side (*dēsiliunt*), where the water tumbles down to form a stream (*rīvōs* 7). Notice the lapping sound of the *l*'s in 15-16.

Discussion

There is a very good, full discussion in K.Quinn: Horace, *The Odes* (Nelson). Others include G.Williams: *The Third Book of Horace's Odes*, OUP and D.West: *Reading Horace*, Edinburgh University Press, pp.128-30.

The poem seems to represent much of what is at the heart of *vita rūstica*: simplicity, awareness of nature and an implicit religious feeling. The formal structure is of a hymn of dedication to a god, here to the *fōns Bandusiae*; there is the traditional invocation in line 1 and the list of the divinity's attributes in 9-12. Quinn sees the poem as a 'dramatic monologue, reproducing the unwinding of the poet's thoughts'. Horace's original touch is to give the reader a series of images - the lusty young goat, the scene of his sacrifice tomorrow as contemplated by the poet and the shade so welcome to animals in the heat of summer. Instead of offerings in the future Horace promises the spring immortality from his poem. This last stanza may be the starting-point for discussion of whether Horace is a true countryman or just rather romantically attached to the images of the country; pupils can be invited to compare modern town-dwellers, many of whom have this idealised conception of idyllic country life.

The editors are indebted to E.J.Kenney for a different interpretation of the poem. Conventionally a poet makes a name *for himself* by imbibing metaphorically from a famous Greek spring associated with poetic inspiration, e.g. Castalia, Hippocrene. In this ode Horace selects a totally obscure Italian spring and makes a name *for it* by writing a poem to it. To Kenney this is the main point of the poem; the rest is decoration.

The sacrifice of the kid presents problems. Some have seen it as being in bad taste. The usual response to this criticism is to point out that animal sacrifice played an important part in ancient religion, as it still does in some modern religions, and to condemn it out of hand is to fail to appreciate its relationship with deep-seated religious beliefs. Yet it was not usual in Roman times for animals to be sacrificed to the spirits of a spring. Why Horace introduced the offering of a kid, in addition to the customary wine and flowers, is something of a mystery. Did he want to emphasise the pathos of the death of a young animal? Or is this qualified by an element of the mock heroic (*et venerem et proelia* and *frūstrā*)? Or is he more concerned to paint a vivid picture of a ritual sacrifice, with the red blood spreading through the clear water? Pupils will no doubt have their own strong opinions.

The town mouse and the country mouse (Horace, *Satires* II.6.79-117)

The passage is from the end of a Satire in which the poet praises the simplicity of country life compared with the pressures of town life; it is put into the mouth of a neighbour who tells the fable to caution those sympathetic to wealth against the extravagance of town life.

Metre: Hexameters

There is a very full treatment of the passage by Tennick, *Libellus Handbook* (CUP), pp.15-23, who quotes a comparable fable by Aesop.

- **2-3** There is clearly a good deal of word-patterning here centring on the two mice. While one can dissect this in literary and linguistic detail, the effect of the pattern is to invite us to contrast the one mouse against the other: each is to be seen in the light of the other in the poem. The 'framing' technique shows this to be the case in each four-word phrase: the country mouse on the outside of the phrase in 2 goes inside in 3 and vice versa with the town mouse.
- **5 quid multa?:** pupils always seem puzzled by this phrase which in full is *quid multa dīcam?* 'Why should I say a lot?'
- **7-8 ferēns** and **dedit** are both to be taken with *āridum...acinum* and *sēmēsa...lardī frusta.*
- **15 carpe viam, mihi crēde, comes:** the dactylic metre enhances *carpe viam*. The sense of *mihi crēde* is colloquial - 'take my advice', 'why don't you?'. The whole phrase is intended to be light-hearted.
- **16-17** By contrast the metre slows down as the town mouse ponderously attempts to reproduce pseudo-Epicurean ideas about mortality.
- **21-2 aventēs...nocturnī subrēpere:** 'eager to creep under (the walls of the city) by night'. The mice are eager to get inside while it is still dark, for security's sake.
- **22ff.** After the journey ends, the vocabulary and ideas become epic as a preparation for the grand meal.
- **25-6 candēret, superessent:** the subjunctives may be generic, 'the sort of house where', or may be used as a stylistic alternative for the indicative.
- **27 canistrīs:** the left-overs from the evening *cēna* were presumably collected in baskets or perhaps left in the baskets in which they had been served.

30 **continuatque dapēs:** the country-mouse has hardly finished one course before the next is brought.
33 **subitō ingēns:** elision conveys the speed of the surprise.
34 **valvārum strepitus:** we are intended to imagine someone coming into the room to clear away the meal. The alliteration of *s, t, c, q,* helps the meaning.
35-6 **currere...trepidāre:** historic infinitives.
36-7 **Molossīs...canibus:** mastiff-type hounds used as watch-dogs. Dactyls suggest fear and speed.
39 **ervō:** the word does service generally for the meagre diet of poor country people.

Discussion

One should resist the temptation to announce at the outset that this is a fable, where the two mice represent town and country dwellers and where the moral is to guard against urban extravagance: that would be to spoil what will be for some a new literary experience in Latin. Teachers will decide for themselves how much of the extract to consider at a time but lines 1-11 or 1-19 are convenient sections to start with; after an initial reading and perhaps translation one could then consider a half-humorous introduction to the discussion, intended to tease out the idea of a fable: 'How did the country mouse come to know the town mouse? How do mice issue invitations? How were the journeys accomplished?' A good deal of fun could be had in seeing how long it takes for the pretence to be seen through - and, of course, some pupils will see it immediately.

The next stage could be an exploration of the human versus the mouse characteristics of the pair: apart from the mice speaking fluent versified Latin they are described in human terms with *amīcus, hospes, pater domūs*; they recline at table, regard a meal as a social occasion and talk about philosophy. What mouse characteristics there are, are not overt and are only what are necessary to establish the pretence: *cavus, dente superbō* and *paleā porrēctus in hornā.* If this is doubted, ask, 'Where are their fur coats and twitching whiskers?' The conclusion is that it is what they represent that matters. Could Horace then have used dung-beetles in his fable? Why are mice attractive characters?

vīta rūstica et vīta urbāna   53

The lesson on extravagance is clearly centred on the two meals and the contrasts to be drawn: the locations (2-3 and 24), the foods on offer (6-8 and 26-7), the hosts (7-8 and 29-31; 10-11 and 28-9) and the guests (8-9 and 32-3). A tabulation of the actual words in two lists on the blackboard might be instructive. This editor cannot agree with those who see the hospitality of the *rūsticus mūs* as meagre and stingy; the description of him in 4-5 seems rather characteristic of those who need to watch the pennies but entertain hospitably, when the occasion demands, as far as they can. Indeed, the idea that *ut...animum* is ironic does not fit easily with the tone of the meal: the chick-pea has been stored up (*sēpositī*) for a special occasion, *āridum... acinum* is a raisin, not a dry grape, and the bacon scraps (*lardī frusta*) represent the pork that was the Italian peasant's staple meat. In eating *ador* and *lolium* he genuinely does leave the better parts of the meal for his guest (11); there is no irony here either. There is more than a passing resemblance to the (admittedly larger-scale) meal offered by Baucis and Philemon to Jupiter and Mercury (Ovid, *Metamorphoses*, Penguin, pp.196-7). There are no details of the town food for us explicitly to criticise but, set against the simplicity of the country meal, its lavishness is implicitly criticised in such vocabulary as *rubrō...coccō, lectōs...eburnōs, purpureā...in veste, praelambēns* as well as the more obvious lines 26-7 and *continuat...dapēs*. The difference in attitude is noted too between the haughty *urbānus* (8-9 where *fastīdia* placed between *variā* and *cēnā* exposes his sheer bad manners towards the best his host can offer) and the hearty enjoyment of the *rūsticus* (32-3).

City extravagance is clearly aimed at (otherwise, why not have the mice visit a country house?); however, let us spare a thought that the *rūsticus* gives up town life when he appreciates the dangers and risks it poses. This theme is not developed (as it is in Aesop's fable) but it is there as a feature. Pupils will enjoy thinking of their own moral.

dē cultū deōrum et vītā hominum

A country festival (Horace, Odes III.18)

Metre: Sapphic

1 **Faune:** a god of the countryside who had certain mystical associations: he had a frightening nature and perhaps was wolf-like and so needed to be appeased (3-4 *lēnis, aequus*). His festival was on 5th December. Horace describes him as a protector of his farm (*Odes* I.17) and of him himself when a falling tree missed him (*Odes* II.17).
fugientum (tē): 'fleeing (from you)'. The description is humorous and refers to Faunus' love of nymphs.

2 **fīnēs:** it is possible this refers to the boundary-stones which marked out property. If it means 'my land', it seems to anticipate *rūra*.

3 **incēdās abeās:** these second person jussive subjunctives will need explanation to pupils.

5 **plēnō...annō:** this refers to the festival in 10. It should be made clear to pupils that this phrase does not imply the end of the calendar year, only that twelve months have elapsed since the last Nones of December.

6-7 **Veneris sodālī...crātērae:** the bowl was used for mixing wine (here plentiful, *larga*) with water. Love and wine, Horace says, go together.

7 **vetus āra:** this implies the altar has been used many times for such festivals; only a small piece of the animal was burnt but the god revelled in the savoury smoke (*multō...odōre*).

10 The Roman method of expressing dates will probably be unfamiliar to pupils; a brief explanation of Kalends, Nones and Ides will suffice here.

13 **audācēs...agnōs:** the lambs are enjoying the holiday atmosphere of the festival and are safe from wolves under the protection of Faunus. The position of *lupus* between *audācēs* and *agnōs* points up the danger; hence the power of Faunus is emphasised.

14 **frondēs:** Horace seems to ask us to believe that the trees are shed-

ding their leaves out of respect for Faunus, to make a carpet for him to walk on.

15-16 The *fossor* is dancing or beating his foot to a rhythm; given his usual occupation of digging up the earth this is humorously viewed as his getting his own back on the land. *ter* implies a three-time rhythm, not stamping his foot three times and no more; the effect is assisted by the alliterative qualities in *pepulisse...pede* and *ter...terram*. There is a contrast between the digger's heavy-footed cavorting and the light feet of the nymphs and Faunus.

Discussion

Horace presents the poem in a hymn format: there is the invocation to Faunus and the brief defining of his rôle in line 1, the request itself in 2-4 and the offering in 5-8. However, the form is used to express the description of a rustic festival on Horace's farm and thus becomes very personal; it also gives the poem an emotional dimension.

We can quickly catch the tone in line 1 where, in place of the standard reciting of the rôles of a god, we have a light-hearted reference to this god's favourite pastime. The first stanza reminds us of the country-dweller's awareness of the powers around him: he needs the cooperation of the gods to ensure the success of his crops and flocks. Thus Horace hopes that Faunus' attendance at his festival will be good-humoured, especially in view of the god's general reputation (see the note on 1 above). The second stanza gives a picture of the ritual, stressing the special nature of the religious occasion and the atmosphere of warm contentment; *larga* is emphatically placed to show that no expense will be spared.

The third and fourth stanzas take us on to the festival itself. Vocabulary is carefully chosen to express happiness, celebration and the (temporary) relief from daily toil: *lūdit* (9), *fēstus, vacat, ōtiōsō* (11), *gaudet* (15). In the last stanza we are reminded of the circumstances behind the festival: at a time when, in ancient Italy, autumn lambing is complete, the god whose rôle is to protect the new-born lambs from wolves is invited to his own festival. Contrary perhaps to our expectations the poem concludes by reverting to the light-hearted tone of 1; however, this ring composition is common in Horace.

The poem gives us glimpses of traditional Roman country religion; we see the essential combination of worship and enjoyment in an uncomplicated setting. Behind it all smiles the face of the poet, the would-be countryman.

One question pupils may like to consider concerns the picture of the wolf among the sheep in 13: does the inclusion of this miraculous element strengthen the tribute to Faunus or does it spoil the cosy, realistic description built up in the rest of the poem?

Recipe for happiness (Martial, Epigrams X.47)

Metre: Hendecasyllables

  2 **Mārtiālis:** this is Iulius Martialis, the poet's closest friend and perhaps patron; he was wealthy and cultivated.
  3 This refers to the snobbery that it was better socially to have inherited wealth than to be a self-made man and also that wealth which came from the land was acceptable, whereas commercial activity was not.
  4-5 *ager* and *focus* characterise country-life, *līs* and *toga* town-life, which normally is not conducive to *mēns quiēta*.
  6 **vīrēs ingenuae:** this is the innate strength of a free-born Roman developed by exercise in the Campus Martius - not the brute strength of a slave, developed by toil.
  7 **prūdēns simplicitās:** one suspects a political comment lies not far beneath the surface - knowing when to be open and frank. An alternative would be to see *prūdēns* applying to the *content* of the plain speech, not to shrewdness about *when* to speak plainly; the thought would then be that it is good to live among people who say what they think and who think sensible things.
  9 The advice here is not to drink to forget one's sorrows but to be able to sleep soundly.
 10 'a wife who's true to you and yet no prude in bed' (Michie, Penguin).
 11 The idea seems to be that you sleep so soundly that morning soon comes. *quī faciat* is a generic subjunctive: 'the sort of sleep that makes the night-time brief'.

12-13 The four subjunctives *velīs, mālīs, metuās, optēs* are probably best treated as jussives: 'you should...'. Pupils will need guidance over *mālīs* (not *malīs*).

Discussion

With the words *vītam...beātiōrem* we ask ourselves, 'happier' than what state of affairs? Alongside the apostrophe of 2 it is tempting to see the poem as pieces of advice to a patron to lead a rather different life. In epigram V.20 (**ōtium,** p.58) Martial rejects the tedious obligations of city life (he mentions *līs* there, too) but seems glad to take part in the busy social round. Perhaps here he goes one stage further: in developing this philosophy there is more of an emphasis on what the country can offer. That apart, the list is fairly standard and delivered in effectively end-stopped lines: there is a hint of resigned acceptance that these are the things which, after all, matter most. His final message is to get on with life day by day, content with what you have. There is a lesson here; who is it intended for? The idea of enjoying life's pleasures, undismayed by the fact that they are transitory, can be usefully contrasted with the ideas in Horace, *Odes* IV.7 in this section. *beātus* had a marked philosophical resonance for Martial's contemporaries; Seneca wrote a treatise *Beata Vita*. Martial may be claiming to be cutting through all the pontificating to give a commonsense view of the happy life. How do pupils react to Martial's vision?

Spring and thoughts of mortality (Horace, *Odes* IV.7)

Metre: First archilochean

1-2 The poem opens with heavy syllables to announce the departure of the winter; the metre then lightens as elements of spring appear in 2.

3-4 The picture is of rivers, once swollen by winter rains, now flowing comfortably within their banks.

6 **nūda**: it is warm enough now to dance naked.

7 **immortālia nē spērēs**: the idea is reinforced by the mainly heavy syllables and by assonance.

9-12 The poet has consciously used a long sense-unit to allow us to appreciate how one season follows inevitably hard on the heels of the last: the four seasons occupy four short clauses and are variously contrasted or linked with each other. Pupils will find the phrase *vēr prōterit aestās interitūra simul...* particularly challenging. Comprehension questions will help: which season tramples on another one? what will summer do? when? and so on.

prōterit is a brutal word. This may reflect the harshness of the Mediterranean summer.

13 **damna...caelestia:** after the basic meaning of the poem is established pupils could be asked to explain the sense of this phrase and then asked if there is any connection between 13 and 9-12 (see Discussion).

14 **nōs:** the emphatic position contrasts the human predicament with the cycle of nature in 13.

17-18 This idea could be compared with those in *Odes* I.11 *carpe diem*.

19 **manūs avidās...hērēdis:** legacy-hunting was common.

23-4 **genus...fācundia...pietās:** pupils need to appreciate how very important all three were to Romans. Torquatus, a shadowy figure, was probably an orator.

25-6 Both Diana and Hippolytus were strongly associated with chastity; Horace's point is that if even Diana cannot restore her favourite, what hope is there for Torquatus after death?

27-8 K.Quinn, *Horace, The Odes* (Nelson) in an excellent note explains that Theseus is imagined as returning to the Underworld and is still there now, unable to free Pirithous. Theseus has no power to remove the chains which have caused his friend to forget (*Lēthaea*). According to Apollodorus (*Epitome* I.24) both were persuaded by Hades to sit on the chair of Lethe to which they were then bound by serpents; there was a famous picture of the two heroes in Hades by Polygnotus. Poets often presuppose readers' familiarity with treatments in art as well as literature. The whole reference here serves as a reminder of what Horace could expect of his readers in the way of picking up recondite allusions. Again, the message for Torquatus is clear.

Discussion

Horace's poem opens with celebration of the arrival of spring; it leads the poet on to the contrast between the regenerative powers of nature, as seen in the cycle of the seasons, and man's mortality. The poem naturally then falls into two parts, although, as will be seen, the point of the division is not incontestable.

An emphatic shout is heard in *diffūgēre nivēs* (1); the rejoicing that spring has come is reflected by the metre in the first two lines. We take *mūtat terra vicēs* (3) at face value - the seasons revolve - and later we give the words an extra significance when man's condition comes into the equation. *immortālia nē spērēs...* (7-8) introduces this wider interpretation, particularly if *spērēs* refers to the reader, to man generally; it seems too early to refer the second person singular to Torquatus who is addressed only in 23. The words additionally prepare for the theme of 9-12: the relentless march of the seasons as reflected in the powerfully on-moving Latin sentence.

We could see the division referred to above at the end of 12: certainly 13 (where *tamen* is significant) announces a clear image of the regenerative element in nature; this leads into the emphatic contrast with man as seen in *nōs* (14). His mortal condition occupies 14-16, concluding with the sombre image of dust and shade. 13-16 are the central four lines of the poem both in thought and mathematically.

It may be better to think of 17-18 as beginning a fresh line of thought. From this point the poem becomes more complex in structure; one has only to re-read lines 1-4 to appreciate their simplicity in contrast with, say, 17-18. Philosophical thoughts of mortality enter; a note of warning is struck (for Torquatus, as it becomes clear) to make the most of one's life, which can end at any time, unlike the natural movement of the year's seasons. Lines 19-20 are the only place in the poem where Horace hints at any regenerative capability for man comparable to that of nature: with *hērēdis* he looks at the inheritance by the next generation only to dismiss it with the words *manūs avidās*; significantly the heir is not explicitly a son or daughter but sounds like a *captātor*, i.e. the idea of man living on in his descendants is being underplayed.

The grim words *cum semel* (21) prepare us for the stark picture of Minos delivering judgement which is *splendida*; pupils will be challenged by the description. The once-for-all nature of death means that Torquatus can never return, underlined by the powerlessness of the earthly-powerful *genus, fācundia* and *pietās* and the anaphora of *nōn* (23-4). Horace uses the colour of mythology to complete the message in 25-8. Pupils may like to discuss why Horace introduces the apparently recondite detail of *Lēthaea* (27). Is it a hint to Torquatus and the reader to expect to be forgotten, to pass as a shade (16) into eternal oblivion and anonymity?

Odes I.4 makes an interesting comparison.

Elysium (Virgil, Aeneid VI.638-65)

This selection of lines has been made by omitting difficult references to individuals as far as possible to leave, it is hoped, a coherent but general picture of the Blessed Groves in Elysium. It is the sight which greets Aeneas and the Sibyl immediately after Aeneas has made his offering of the Golden Bough to Proserpina at the palace door.

Metre: Hexameters

- 3-4 **largior...purpureō:** the composite picture of the aether and its light invests the scene in a golden haze reminiscent of Turner.
- 4 **suum, sua:** pupils will need guiding towards a meaning of 'their own...and not ours': we do not see their sun and stars.

    nōrunt: this difficult change to a plural subject could refer to 'plains' or to 'they (the Blessed)'.
- 6 The metre of the line is spondaic to reflect the effort of sport.
- 7 Here the metre is built around three successive pairs of dactyls and spondees to suggest the rhythm of the dancing and singing. The effect is enhanced by the alliteration of '*p*' and other consonants.
- 9 **nātī meliōribus annīs:** the sense is, 'born in the Heroic Age'.
- 10-13 Peace has come through the redundancy of the trappings of war but the qualities of men observed in war have followed them to the grave. There may be a hint of irony here.
- 14 **manus...passī:** *passī* agrees with the plural sense of the collective *manus*.
- 19 **vittā:** the woollen head-band marked out those who had special

dē cultū deōrum et vītā hominum 61

religious significance, here priests and those who had contributed particular service in life.

Discussion

Virgil's atmospheric picture is a version of the traditional view of life after death in the Underworld. It is noticeably less gloomy than Homer's, which is the place for all mortals who have died. Virgil's Elysium welcomes the seemingly very large number of those who have led worthwhile lives: although heroes predominate in this selection, a very wide cross-section is implied in 17-18. The light is bright (3-4) and the atmosphere optimistic (5-7). Pupils will need to be reminded of Tartarus, Virgil's abode for the wicked; they could be invited to read the Sibyl's description of it to Aeneas just before this passage (Penguin, pp.163-6). They will probably raise the question of the judgement of souls, too.

The impressionistic picture, where form and structure are less important than light and atmosphere, leaves some questions unanswered: why do dead horses graze? what sun and stars? The words *hīc...hīc...hīc* (3, 8, 14) take us on a tour, picking out the highlights: peace and contentment (10-13) with the subtle pathos of old soldiers behaving as when alive (*vīvīs*), servants of the state (14-16) with more pathos (*dum vīta manēbat*) and the virtuous rewarded (17-19). But the overall effect is one of a blended picture, not one of sharply focused, separate scenes.

There is ample opportunity here for comparison with the beliefs of modern faiths concerning life after death. Do pupils find Virgil's picture more attractive than the traditional picture of Heaven - long white robes, the playing of harps, the scene located somewhere in the sky?

Live now! (Martial, *Epigrams* I.15.11-12)

Metre: Elegiac couplet

    1 **nōn est...sapientis:** the genitive of characteristic will probably be unfamiliar.

    2 **vīve hodiē:** the elision brings both words into one foot for emphasis. These two lines come at the end of a twelve-line poem, written to Iulius Martialis (an old and wealthy patron) who is advised to get on with living

his life to the full, seizing life's joys with both hands. These two lines encapsulate the familiar motif of 'live for today'; the idea is given bite by the epigrammatic form which contrasts *vīvam* with *vīve* and can leave *hodiē* till last. V.20 (in the ōtium section) and X.47 in this section are also addressed to Martialis.

It would be a good exercise to ask pupils to pick out the lines of Horace's *diffūgēre nivēs* in this section which correspond most closely to these two lines.

The only form of immortality (Seneca, 415 in *Anthologia Latina* I.1, ed. D.R.Shackleton Bailey)

Metre: Elegiac couplet

1 **fātō:** perhaps most easily explained by recourse to the three Fates, one of whom cut the thread of life at death.

These are the last two lines of a poem which deals with the commonplace that time will destroy all the greatest monuments of man. The idea that literature alone survives to perpetuate man's memory is frequent in Latin; Homer here serves only as an example. Similar thoughts will be found in Horace, *Odes* III.30 and in the epilogue to Ovid's *Metamorphoses*. Among passages in Pliny are I.3, II.10, III.7, V.5 (end), VII.33.

The poet's advice to mourners (Lucretius, *De Rerum Natura* III.894-903)

Metre: Hexameters

1 Three long syllables stress the intensity of the message to come.

2-3 **nec dulcēs occurrent ōscula nātī praeripere:** 'nor will your dear children run to meet you to kiss you eagerly'.

4-5 **nōn poteris factīs flōrentibus esse tuīsque praesidium:** the translation in the pupil's text is preferable to the more conventional interpretation, 'you will not be able to be prosperous and a protection to your family', where *factīs flōrentibus* would be a strange descriptive ablative after *esse*.

5 **miserō miserē:** the wordplay is clear but there is also the effective repetition of the mournful sounding letter 'm' in the line too.

adēmit: the verb uses dative case (*miserō...tibī*) of the person from whom something is taken. Pupils could compare *voler à quelqu'un* in French.

7 **illud:** this prospective use ('the following') will be unfamiliar: 'what they don't add in this situation is...'.

7-8 **nec...ūnā:** this difficult sentence becomes easier if *super* is taken closely with *insidet* and if *ūnā* is understood to imply 'together with you in the grave'.

Discussion

It is important to establish the context of this extract from the outset: Lucretius imagines the mourners at a funeral to be addressing the dead man, 'quoting' their words with *aiunt* (1-6); Lucretius retorts with thoughts of his own on what they do not say (7-8). Lines 9-10 form a comment by the poet.

The poem opens with traditional feelings of mourners; there are rhetorical features here to enhance the lines (*iam iam* 1, *miserō miserē* 5, and the alliteration in 6, and the words which remind one of funeral speeches or tombstone inscriptions: *laeta uxor, dulcēs nātī* 1-2). The poet sets this up so that he can then reject it in the last four lines.

There is a sense in which Lucretius is mocking these views but the mockery is not overt - certainly not on the evidence of so few lines. Some conversely may feel there to be very real pathos. The passage comes after a section in which the poet argues that in death the unique combination of mind and body which gave life to the person is broken; hence death denies existence in any form and cannot harm us. The living attribute their own feelings to a vision of the dead, he argues, and therein lies the error. The mourners do not perceive that the dead can have no longing for the good memories of life; if the mourners only realised this they would be less anguished. Death is final: no consciousness survives. A question for pupils to consider is whether the mourners' speech in 1-6 is a piece of ridiculous sentimentality or a touching lament, appropriate to the occasion; which words and phrases lead them to their opinion? Do pupils feel that Lucretius really addresses the problem of grief and loss felt by the bereaved; how consoling is his 'reply' to the mourners?

COMMENTARY: PROSE SELECTIONS

Germānicus et Pīsō

The pupil's text has been distilled from the much more detailed account given by Tacitus in Books II (from Chapter 55) and III (Chapters 1-15). The following notes owe much to the editions of H.Furneaux (*The Annals of Tacitus*, OUP) and D.C.Chandler (*Selections from Annals II-III, Germanicus and Piso*, CUP).

Germanicus was the nephew of Tiberius and adopted by him in AD 4. In the following year he married Agrippina, the granddaughter of Augustus.

Piso in Syria

1 **cōnsilia:** these are his plans to thwart Germanicus.

2 **legiōnēs:** as *lēgātus* or governor of Syria (an imperial province), Piso would automatically have control over the four legions stationed there. The main role of the legions was to guard against attack from Parthia.

2-3 **largītiōne...iūvābat:** his intention was to win the support of the more disreputable elements in the army by means of bribery. Tacitus' condemnation of Piso's behaviour is shown by his use of pejorative words: *largītiōne, ambitū, licentiam, lascīvientēs.*

3-4 **cum veterēs...dēmōvisset:** the experienced and disciplined officers would have opposed Piso's will.

4 **clientibus:** Piso's clients, or hangers-on, would have obeyed him without question. The main purposes of the changes he made to the army were, firstly, to transfer the loyalty of the legions from Germanicus to himself; he could then deny Germanicus their support. Secondly, he wanted the army to make itself unpopular in the province. By these means he could hope to secure his second objective, to make Germanicus' task of achieving a peaceful settlement in the East as difficult as possible. In the event, Piso proved a poor judge of the situation, since the soldiers were unlikely to turn

Germānicus et Pīsō 65

against so popular a leader as Germanicus, who was, in any case, nominally Piso's superior.

5-6 **dēsidiam...sinēbat:** there are two examples here of *variatio*, a feature of Tacitus' narrative style: firstly, two abstract objects and one personal with *sinēbat*; secondly, of three prepositional phrases, two are introduced by *in* and one by *per*.

6 **Plancīna:** she came from a noble and wealthy family, a fact which increased Piso's arrogance. According to Tacitus (II.43), she had been prevailed upon by the jealous Empress Livia to persecute Agrippina. The hostile Tacitus consistently presents Plancina as the opposite of Agrippina.

7 **exercitiō equitum intererat:** the general's wife had no official position in the Roman army, so her presence at military exercises was a breach of discipline.

9-10 **instantior cūra:** Armenia lay along the borders of the Roman empire, acting as a buffer zone between Rome and the ever-hostile Parthia. Tiberius' policy was to establish a pro-Roman king on the throne of Armenia as quickly as possible, before Parthia could orchestrate enough support for her candidate.

The death of Germanicus

11-12 **saevam...acceptī:** 'his belief that poison had been received from Piso increased the terrible virulence of the illness'. There is no evidence beyond Tacitus' persuasive rhetoric of Piso's complicity in Germanicus' death. The accounts of the human remains, spells and curses found in Germanicus' house could have been fabricated as evidence against Piso.

12 **ērutae:** this may be taken with *solō ac parietibus* 'dug up from the floor and walls' or by itself 'the disinterred remains'; the latter is perhaps the more effective. Human remains were often used in magic.

13 **carmina:** spells in verse, whereas *dēvōtiōnēs* could be in verse or prose. Many lead curse tablets survive; for further information on curses, see *Cambridge Latin Course* Unit IIIA, Stage 22 and Teacher's Handbook pp.21-3.

14-15 cinerēs sēmustī: these were half-burned and *tābō oblitī* because they were snatched from the funeral pyre.

15 crēditur: 'it is believed'; the use of this word suggests that Tacitus himself did not believe in magic.

16 ā Pīsōne: to be taken with *missī*.

17 incūsābantur quod...exspectārent: 'were being accused of awaiting...', *lit.* 'were being blamed because (it was said that) they were waiting'. *exspectārent*: subjunctive because the reason was alleged.

18 haud minus īrā quam per metum: 'as much in anger as through fear'; note the *variatio*.

19 compōnit: historic present; note the emphatic position to suggest an immediate response.

amīcitiam...renūntiābat: the 'friendship' was of course the formal diplomatic relationship expected of officials serving in the same province. Germanicus' renunciation of this relationship was therefore tantamount to dismissing Piso from office. The imperfect tense may be conative: 'he tried to renounce'. There was a rumour that Germanicus ordered Piso to leave the province; that he did leave Syria is clear from 44, where we learn that he had reached Cos, five hundred miles away in the direction of Rome.

20-1 Germānicus...aderat: note how the apparent improvement and final decline are compressed: the event is less important to Tacitus than the reactions of everyone around.

22 erit vōbīs occāsiō: he uses the future as a polite imperative to remind his friends of their duty.

22-3 querendī...lēgēs: Germanicus does not ask his friends to seek to bring the murderer to justice by petitioning the emperor, whom he suspected of some measure of complicity; instead, he tells them to raise the matter in the senate where they might receive a more sympathetic hearing.

24 ignāvō questū: lamentation will not benefit the dead, and so will be futile; it also requires less effort of will to mourn than to pursue justice. Action is needed!

26 fortūnam meam: Germanicus is probably referring to the combination of rank and successful career, which has made him the most popular member of the imperial family.

27 **ultiōnem:** '(the pursuit of) revenge'.

29 **neque multō post:** 10 October, AD 19.
ingentī lūctū prōvinciae: 'amid the great grief of the province'. Tacitus is emphasising the grief of the people of Syria in order to build up the pathos of Germanicus' death.

30-1 **circumiacentium...rēgēsque:** the extent of the lamentation is again emphasised, this time by the vague generalisations suggesting a wide geographical area. The 'surrounding peoples' would probably include neighbouring territories under Roman control, while the 'foreign nations' would include Parthia, whose king, according to Suetonius (*Gaius* 5), suspended hunting out of respect.

31-2 **cōmitās...hostēs:** both allies and enemies had cause to respect Germanicus.

34-5 **genus locumque mortis:** the cause of Alexander's death was also uncertain, with rumours of poison. Alexander died at Babylon; this was a long way from Antioch, where Germanicus died, but to a Roman reader both would seem remote cities on or beyond the eastern boundary of the empire.

35 **adaequārent:** generic subjunctive. Tacitus probably introduces this comparison to exaggerate the esteem in which Germanicus was held.

36 **genere īnsignī ortum:** Alexander was the son of King Philip of Macedon.
vix trīgintā annōs: Alexander died at the age of 32, Germanicus at 33.

Mourning

39 **morārentur:** generic subjunctive.

40 **cum cineribus Germānicī et līberīs:** Tacitus focuses on the most poignant images during the departure, to increase the sympathy of the reader (cf. *fērālēs reliquiās sinū ferret* in 43).

41-3 **miserantibus...ferret:** Tacitus brings out the contrast between her previous good fortune and her current (*tunc*) wretchedness and vulnerability.

45 quō gāvīsus: note the stark contrast between Piso's reaction and the plight of Agrippina.

caedit victimās: the slaughter of victims (in thanksgiving) would have been extraordinarily tactless of Piso, considering the high status and popularity of Germanicus.

47-8 īnsolēscit Plancīna...mūtāvit: at first glance, it appears that Plancina was even more insensitive than her husband to the general grief felt for Germanicus, in choosing this very moment to emerge from mourning for her dead sister into bright clothes and jewels; doubtless this is what Tacitus wishes us to believe. It is, however, perfectly possible that her period of mourning had just ended when news of Germanicus' death arrived; Piso's sacrifices and temple visits could equally have been to mark the end of the mourning. Such a coincidence would have been quickly seized on by Piso's enemies.

49 at Rōmae: we now move back in time to the period of Germanicus' sickness. The fact that the reader knows that at the time of the rumours he was already dead lends dramatic irony to this scene. Tacitus wishes to establish from the outset that public sentiment was firmly on the side of Germanicus.

50-1 cūncta...adferēbantur: 'everything was being reported with the pessimistic exaggeration usually applied to news from afar'. Tacitus supports his statement about this particular occasion with a disputable generalisation.

51 dolor, īra, questūs ērumpēbant: note the rapid progression of reactions to the news.

52 extrēmās, relēgātum: emotive words distorting the truth but giving a likely representation of popular opinion.

52-3 ideō Pīsōnī permissam prōvinciam: Piso immediately becomes the scapegoat. Note the striking alliteration.

53-4 hōs vulgī sermōnēs...incendit: 'so inflamed this kind of talk among the people'.

55 sūmptō iūstitiō: since the *iūstitium* was a standard expression of public mourning, it was usual to announce it by official edict after confirmation of death. On this occasion, the outburst of public grief is spontaneous.

56 **clauderentur domūs:** i.e. the private houses of the wealthy were closed to all *clientēs*.

56-7 **silentium et gemitus:** i.e. in the absence of all the usual sounds of business there was silence, broken only by lamentation.

59 **nāvigātiōne...intermissā:** the narrative returns to Agrippina's journey to Rome, which she is so anxious to complete in her desire for revenge that she even sails in winter, when sailing was normally curtailed.

60 **Brundisiō:** Brundisium was (and is) the main seaport for travel to and from Greece and further east.

61-2 **mīlitēs quī...stīpendia fēcerant:** veterans from Germanicus' campaigns in Germany.

64-5 **silentiōne...exciperent:** deliberative subjunctive: 'whether to receive her in silence or with words of some kind as she disembarked'.

66 **ut solet:** sailors were normally only too happy to reach their destination safely.

67 **duōbus...līberīs:** one of them, Gaius (Caligula), was to be the next emperor.

68 **ēgressa...oculōs:** by making *dēfīxit* the finite verb rather than *ēgressa (est)*, Tacitus focuses attention on the emotive detail; indeed, the whole sentence is designed to maximise the pathos.

68-9 **īdem fuit omnium gemitus:** this is the climax of the whole paragraph: Tacitus wishes the reader to visualise the scene as one from a Greek tragedy, the onlookers playing the role of the chorus. As Chandler says, 'Agrippina's disembarkation is stage-managed for maximum effect, but is the stage-manager Agrippina or Tacitus?' The dignified bearing of Agrippina would have a greater impact on a Roman than uncontrolled distress.

Revenge

70 **diē senātūs:** 'on the day of the senate's meeting'.

71 **patris meī:** Tiberius is referring here to Augustus, not his real father.

lēgātus: Augustus had appointed Piso governor of Nearer Spain.
71-2 **Germānicō adiūtōrem:** this sounds rather disingenuous.
74-5 **utrum Pīsō...exstīnxerit:** an important distinction: if the first and lesser charge were proved, Tiberius (as the unquoted part of his speech makes clear) would renounce his ties of friendship with Piso; if the more serious charge of murder were proved, Piso would be condemned.
76 **ad sēditiōnem:** this is a third charge against Piso that the senate would have to consider.
77 **statuitur:** this verb is used with two meanings: firstly, '(a period of two days) was allocated'; secondly, 'it was decreed that...'.
78 **intervallum:** presumably to give the defence time to prepare its arguments.
80-1 **mīlitēs...corrūpisse:** the friends of Germanicus press the third charge of treason first.
81 **sociōrum iniūriās:** 'ill-treatment of the people of the province'; see 5-6.
83 **sacra et immolātiōnēs:** see 45-6.
84 **petīvisse armīs rem pūblicam:** 'had made war on the state'.
85 **in cēterīs crīminibus:** i.e. the charges of treason and abuse of Germanicus.
86 **ambitiō mīlitum:** see 2-3.
87-8 **sōlum...dīluere:** the defence had to concentrate on refuting the main charge of murder, and had the best chance of success because of the absence of positive evidence of poison. However, Piso's position was still difficult because Germanicus' death remained suspicious, the charge of treason was upheld, and a hostile mob was making itself heard outside the senate-house, threatening Piso with death.
89-90 **sī Pīsō...ēvāsisset:** i.e. if he were acquitted.
91 **Plancīnae invidia:** 'ill-feeling towards Plancina'. The fate of Plancina, as Piso's partner in guilt, is as important to Tacitus as Piso's own.
91-2 **dum Pīsōnī...absolūtiōnis:** Tacitus must be taking the narrative back to a time before the trial of Piso had reached its climax.

93 **comitem exitiī:** 'his companion in death'.
94 **paulātim sēgregārī:** i.e. over the next two or three days she slowly withdrew her support, the better to save herself.
94-5 **quod postquam...intellēxit:** 'since Piso saw that this (i.e. Plancina's desertion) meant the end for him'. Plancina had been Piso's best hope of a pardon, because she was a friend of the powerful Empress Livia (Tiberius' mother), who hated Agrippina. As it happened, Plancina gained a pardon for herself, perhaps at the expense of abandoning Piso.
96 **in posterum diem:** 'for the following day'.
97 **pauca scrībit:** i.e. he wrote what were thought to be notes for the next day's defence.
98 **solita...exsequitur:** i.e. he bathed and had dinner.
99 **ēgressā...uxōre:** Plancina adds physical to spiritual and moral separation, completing Piso's isolation.
100-1 **prīmā lūce...repertus est:** a laconic but effective record of the final episode.

Discussion

The story of Germanicus and Piso provides a rich source for discussion. The characters of the antagonists, the contrast between their wives, the attitude of Tiberius, the interplay of historical fact and rumour or supposition, the extent of Tacitus' literary licence and political bias, are all important for our understanding of the events but are elusive. It is also worth noting that Tacitus wrote this in AD 112, long after the events.

Of Germanicus' popularity among the soldiers and common people of Rome and Asia there can be little doubt. His abilities as a general and administrator are more questionable, since he achieved little of lasting significance, and apparently attached more importance to sight-seeing in Egypt than starting work. It is quite possible that Tiberius had good reason to send Piso to keep an eye on Germanicus in the East.

Despite Tacitus' overt hostility towards Piso, there is considerable evidence to suggest that he was an able man of very distinguished family, with enough attributes to have induced Augustus to have looked upon him as his heir at one time. As for the accusations of treason against him, much depends on the perspective adopted. He certainly stirred up a brief and ineffectual civil war in Syria in trying to win back the control of the province after Germanicus' death. It could be argued, however, that he had been illegally expelled by Germanicus and that the man appointed by Germanicus to succeed him as governor was in illegal possession. Tacitus does not tell us Piso's motives behind his actions, probably because he did not know them. Much hinges on the secret instructions given to Piso by Tiberius when he dispatched him as governor 'to help Germanicus'; if his brief really was to kill Germanicus and to obstruct his activities in the East, then Piso had carried out his orders effectively. Unfortunately for Piso, the popularity of Germanicus and Agrippina was so great that he found himself at once the focus of popular hatred, which Tiberius could not ignore. We shall probably never know whether Tiberius accepted the verdict of Piso's trial as fair or as a means of covering his own guilt, just as we shall never know the real cause of Germanicus' death.

Pupils might like to discuss the theatrical presentation of Agrippina's return to Rome with the ashes of her husband, and the harsh contrast made by the inopportune rejoicing of Plancina and her husband. The final desertion of Piso by Plancina is similarly appropriate in confirming his ultimate isolation. Are these scenes anything more than a manipulation of the facts by Tacitus in order to prejudice the reader against what he saw as a repugnant imperial court?

A good way into discussion is to pose the question 'Who killed Germanicus?' Pupils are then likely, sooner or later, to raise for themselves the question of Tacitus' reliability. If they are asked 'Does Tacitus ever state that Piso murdered Germanicus?' they are sometimes surprised, on looking back over the text, to see that the answer is unequivocally 'no'. The supplementary question 'Why is it then, that so many readers are left with the impression that Piso *did* murder Germanicus, and at the emperor's bidding, too?' can lead on to such topics as the references to hearsay, the use of innuendo, and Tacitus' employment of a magnificent and tendentious literary technique.

Some pupils will enjoy the account of the death of Germanicus and trial of Piso in Chapters 20 and 21 (with a later surprise in Chapter 29) of *I, Claudius* by Robert Graves.

Messalīna (Extracts from Tacitus, *Annals* XI.12-13, 26-38)

The affair between Messalina and Silius began in AD 47 and was brought to an end in the following year; more precise dating is not possible. This is a much-shortened version of the episode, which Tacitus regarded as of sufficient importance to merit fourteen chapters of Book XI.

Adultery

2 **C. Sīlium:** Silius was the consul designate.
3 **Iūniam Sīlānam:** she died in exile.
4 **exturbāret:** the subject of this verb is Messalina; this is more effective than simply stating that Silius divorced his wife.
  līberō: 'without a wife'.
  adulterō: predicative: 'as her adulterous lover'.
4-5 **neque...nescius erat:** i.e. Silius was all too aware of the public scandal and the personal danger that would inevitably result from an affair with the emperor's wife.
5-6 **exitium...fore certum:** such was the power and selfishness of Messalina that she would have had no hesitation in denouncing Silius if he refused her advances.
6-7 **nōnnūllam...spem esse:** i.e. if he acquiesced, he had a good chance of avoiding detection.
7 **simul...magna praemia:** Messalina, partly at least because of her official status, had access to vast wealth and would be generous to her lover; she might also help to advance his career (see note on 10 below).
9 **ventitat domum:** 'repeatedly visited his house'.
  ēgredientī: 'whenever he appeared in public'.
10 **dat opēs honōrēsque:** both constituted an abuse of her position: the wealth and possessions legally belonged to her husband, and the honours, which presumably took the form of public office and status (his designation to the consulship and his elevation to the patrician status may have been gifts from Messalina), were the emperor's to give, not hers.

74 Commentary: prose selections

12 mātrimōniī suī ignārus: 'was unaware of the state of his marriage'.

13 iam: we are to understand that the affair has continued in the manner described into the following year (AD 48), unknown to Claudius. Messalina, becoming bored with mere adultery, now wished for new excitement.

facilitātem: because it was no longer a challenge or a novelty.

adulteriōrum: it is uncertain whether the plural indicates a Tacitean exaggeration or a series of adulterous relationships.

14 sīve...an: although this is the only occurrence in Tacitus of this combination (standing for *sīve...sīve*), he is here following his usual practice of placing second the alternative which he himself prefers.

14-15 ipsa perīcula...ratus: 'thinking the dangers themselves to be the remedy against imminent dangers'. This is typical of Tacitus' epigrammatic style. The intended meaning is slightly akin to our proverb, 'attack is the best form of defence'. His plan was nothing less than the removal of Claudius; once this was accomplished, there would be less likelihood of anyone trying to punish Silius, especially if he could use his proposed marriage to Messalina as a stepping-stone to the throne.

15-16 abrumpī...urgēbat: this is the only occurrence of this verb with accusative and infinitive to express an indirect command.

16 quippe: used to introduce his arguments to Messalina.

nōn exspectandum: impersonal passive. Silius is urging Messalina to plot the deposition and probably the murder of the emperor.

17 caelibem: he had been forced to divorce his wife (cf. 1-4 above); probably Tacitus intends a certain irony to be seen in this use of the word here.

17-18 nūptiīs...parātum: he was ready to marry Messalina and adopt Britannicus (and presumably Octavia, the sister of Britannicus, as well); both of these acts could legally take place only after the death or divorce of Claudius.

18-19 eandem...potentiam: because she would still be the wife of an emperor (Silius).

19 additā sēcūritāte: 'and her safety would be more secure'.

20 **insidiīs incautus:** i.e. he took a long time to realise his danger when someone plotted against him.
ad īram celer: i.e. once he had become aware of the deception.
21 **amōre:** causal ablative: 'not through any love for her husband'.
21-2 **verita...sperneret:** Messalina liked the idea of marriage, but was unsure, for selfish reasons, of the wisdom of allowing Silius to usurp the throne.
23 **persuāsum (est):** impersonal passive.
nōmen...mātrimōniī: it could only be a nominal marriage, because she had not gained a divorce from her husband.
23-4 **ob magnitūdinem īnfāmiae:** it was the sheer outrageousness of the idea that appealed to her.
24 **nec ultrā...quam dum:** 'waiting only until'.
25 **sacrificiī grātiā:** Claudius was *pontifex maximus* and so would have overseen important sacrifices. This particular sacrifice was connected either with a grain shortage or with the dedication of a temple he had built at Ostia.

Messalina is denounced

27 **domus prīncipis:** all the members of the imperial staff.
27-8 **eī quī potentiam habēbant:** the freedmen who were Claudius' closest advisers and who had most to lose from a coup.
29-30 **sī...persuāsissent:** pluperfect subjunctive in indirect statement (for a future perfect in the original *oratio recta*): 'they hoped that if...'.
30 **sine quaestiōne:** a trial would have brought unwelcome publicity as well as a delay, which would have given Messalina time to win Claudius round.
31 **nē ille dēfēnsiōnem audīret:** the first danger was that Claudius might be exposed to Messalina's attempts to argue her innocence; Claudius was gullible and weak-willed enough to be persuaded by her.
32 **nēve clausae aurēs...nōn essent:** 'or that his ears would not be closed to her even if she confessed'; i.e. even if she confessed her adultery, there was every chance that Claudius would listen to her pleas and excuses and so fail to take action against her. This second danger,

Commentary: prose selections

combined with the first, led to the plan to keep Messalina away from Claudius.

Narcissus: Claudius' principal secretary in charge of his correspondence; because of the power he exercised in this position, he is often mentioned by Tacitus.

33 **occāsiōnēs:** i.e. opportunities to present a convincing case of Messalina's guilt to Claudius (cf. 29-30).

34 **duās eius paelicēs:** i.e. two of the emperor's freedwomen kept by him as courtesans. Narcissus must have thought that Claudius would be more likely to believe women who enjoyed his intimacy but had no political advantage to gain, rather than himself, whose influence was dependent on the emperor's favour.

prōmissīs: these included the assurance of their own increased influence with the emperor once his wife was removed.

35 **Calpurnia:** nothing is known of this woman.

39 **discidiumne tuum...nōvistī:** 'do you know that you are divorced?'

40 **populus et senātus et mīlitēs:** i.e. the plebs, the senate and the Praetorian Guard (in ascending order of importance in the eyes of Claudius, who had been chosen by the praetorians to become emperor after the murder of Caligula). This neat tricolon embraces the whole population of Rome - save the emperor himself.

40-1 **nisi...agis, tenet urbem marītus:** i.e. 'without prompt action, your wife's husband will quickly be master of Rome'. The present stands for the immediate future. It is used idiomatically in the protasis of conditionals to express threat or warning. Its use in the apodosis is particularly Tacitean.

42 **rūmor:** almost a Virgilian personification.

43 **venīre:** i.e. he was on his way back from Ostia to Rome, which he would have to cross to visit the praetorian camp, situated on the northeastern outskirts.

44 **adferrent:** subjunctive to express purpose after *quī*.

44-5 **Lūculliānōs...hortōs:** these gardens had recently been acquired by Messalina after contriving the death of their previous owner.

46 **rēs adversae...eximerent:** i.e. her course of action was instinctive.

47 **aspicī ā marītō**: in the belief that Claudius' attitude towards her would soften once she was in a position to work on his emotions.

48-9 **in complexum patris īrent**: his own children by Messalina could be expected to soften his heart; children need a living mother.

50-1 **per urbem**: i.e. from the gardens of Lucullus in the north of the city to the *Porta Ostiensis* to the south, at which point she climbed on a garden refuse cart.

51-2 **vehiculō...ēripiuntur**: so low has she fallen. It is even possible that Tacitus likens her to the refuse being ejected from the city.

53 **praevalēbat**: 'had more weight in their minds'.

54 **clāmitābat**: the use of the frequentative and of the imperfect tense suggests the insistent nature of her demands.

56 **Sīlium...referēns**: Narcissus is determined that the sight of Claudius' wife and her mention of their children should be trumped by reminders of her adultery, not only with Silius but with many others.

cōdicillōs...indicēs: it is unclear whether this is some kind of documentary proof of Messalina's adultery, or simply a list of names or accusations written down by Narcissus to impress Claudius with his wife's guilt. In either case, the intention was to divert Claudius' attention away from his family.

58 **offerēbantur**: 'were being brought forward'; the imperfect indicates an action which was attempted but not completed: Narcissus was too quick for them.

The death of Messalina

60 **libertō**: Narcissus. The relationship is an inversion of the norm.

61 **in castrīs**: the praetorian camp mentioned above.

62 **praemonente Narcissō**: Narcissus had sought and been given by Claudius temporary command of the Praetorian Guard, in the belief that this would increase his prospects of overthrowing Messalina. Claudius was doubtless glad to be relieved of the main burden of dealing with the Guard, since he was feeling far from resolute. Probably *praemonente* here signifies that Narcissus warned the

soldiers that a crisis was imminent, before leaving the emperor to
supply details.

63-4 nōmina...flāgitantium: presumably Narcissus gave only an outline
of the plot at first, in order to keep Messalina's name concealed,
fearing that the soldiers would be overawed by her powerful
position and be unwilling to act; once their passions had been
roused by general warnings of imminent rebellion against the
emperor, they would be less likely to subside when the identities
were revealed.

64 ductus Sīlius ad tribūnal: Tacitus speeds up the action here: the
arrest of Silius is omitted. The *tribūnal* was the raised platform
which was a standard feature of the *prīncipia* (headquarters) of a
fort; here the commanding officer addressed his soldiers. Now
Silius faced Narcissus. Probably Narcissus dealt with Silius first
because he knew the Guard would have no compunction about
executing him, whereas they might balk at killing the empress.

65 precātus est...accelerārētur: Silius realised that his situation was
hopeless when he saw that Claudius, Narcissus and the Praetorian
Guard were all ranged against him. Tacitus does not even trouble
to recount his death. (The normal penalty for treason against the
emperor was beheading.)

66 Lūculliānīs in hortīs: Messalina has returned there from the *via
Ostiēnsis* as her one remaining refuge.

66, 67 prōlātāre, compōnere: pupils will probably not have met the historic infinitive.

67 compōnere precēs: she 'was composing a letter of appeal' to Claudius.

spē et īrā: her hope is to be pardoned and, perhaps, to take ven-
geance on Narcissus, against whom the *īra* was particularly directed. This sentence shows a typical Tacitean economy of expression, enhanced by the historic infinitives.

tantam superbiam: these words are balanced by *nihil honestum* in
83.

69 vertisset: intransitive here.

71 fēmina misera: 'the poor woman'. Claudius is beginning to weaken.

72 **causam dīcendam:** this is precisely what Narcissus has striven to avoid.
74 **sī morārētur:** i.e. if he delayed getting rid of Messalina.
propinquam noctem: night-time would bring back softer memories of Messalina to Claudius.
76 **centuriōnibus et tribūnō:** these were the officers stationed at the palace to guard the emperor while he was in residence. *quī aderat* suggests that it was only by chance that a higher ranking officer than a centurion was on hand to supervise the execution.
exsequī: a rare use of the infinitive with *dēnūntiō* in an indirect command.
76-7 **ita imperātōrem iubēre:** the soldiers would not undertake such a task without believing that they had the emperor's authority. It is important to appreciate the enormous risk Narcissus is running in claiming the emperor's authority for his order. Why did he feel he could get away with it?
77 **ūnus ē lībertīs:** one of the imperial freedmen, who could be counted on to obey Narcissus and see that Messalina did not escape and that the sentence was carried out. Narcissus was afraid that at the last moment the soldiers would balk at the task.
78-9 **humī fūsam:** 'prostrate on the ground'.
79 **māter Lepida:** Domitia Lepida, great-niece of Augustus and cousin of Agrippina, Nero's mother, who later engineered Lepida's death.
79-80 **haud concors:** this was because Messalina had brought about the death of her mother's second husband, Appius Silanus.
80 **suprēmīs...necessitātibus:** 'in her final extremity'.
81 **suādēbat:** either conative imperfect: 'tried to persuade her' or iterative imperfect: 'kept urging her'.
nē percussōrem opperīrētur: that it was a less ignoble death to take one's own life was a widely held and, during these times, widely practised belief.
83-4 **sed nihil...corruptō:** even at this final crisis in her life, Tacitus does not shrink from attacking Messalina's character and accusing her of cowardice. (This is in contrast to the way he treats other ignoble

characters, such as Vitellius.)
85 **cum...pulsae sunt:** indicative with 'inverse' *cum*.
87 **ferrum...accēpit:** 'took a dagger'.
87-8 **iugulō aut pectorī:** 'now to her throat, now to her breast'.
88 **per trepidātiōnem:** 'in terror'.

Discussion

There is no doubt that Tacitus was a moralist who deplored the decadence of this period, particularly evident in the imperial families. Messalina was a prime example of such corruption, which, if we are to believe Tacitus, afflicted women at least as much as men. To whom do we attach the greater blame for the adulterous relationship between Messalina and Silius? Tacitus portrays the latter almost as the victim, forced to divorce his own wife and unable to refuse Messalina for fear of his life; only later, when it was too late to back out, did Silius take the lead.

For most of the episode, Tacitus is content to leave judgement of Messalina to the reader, since he ensures that her guilt emerges clearly from her actions. Occasionally, however, he passes judgement himself, as in 23-4, 67-8 and 83-4. Whereas under any other circumstances we might be expected to recoil in horror from the picture of a defenceless woman being butchered without even a fair trial, here Tacitus is confident that we shall regard her death as entirely justified.

The discussion could be further extended by asking the question: 'Does Tacitus attack Messalina because she was a woman?' There was a long tradition in the Judaeo-pagan world of stories showing prejudice against women, e.g. Eve, Potiphar's wife, Phaedra, the woman of Ephesus. Can Tacitus be seen to share this prejudice?

Another fruitful topic for students to discuss is characterisation; this should be done with close reference to the text. The main characters - Messalina, Silius, Claudius, Narcissus - are all vividly drawn. Messalina, as well as being morally corrupt, is a manipulator with a good understanding of psychology: she knows that Claudius is too weak to withstand her charms. Silius takes life - and death - as they come; his plot against the emperor was apparently serious, but we are not told whether his main motive was political or sexual. Claudius, who as emperor ought to be the fountainhead of power, is instead weak, unable to make up his mind, unaware of what is happening around him and a prey to stronger influences. Narcissus, whom we might have expected to see as a villain, is placed on the side of moral rectitude, even though he is at the same time protecting his own position. An interesting point is the great disparity in age between Messalina and Claudius: in AD 47, when her affair with Silius began, Messalina was about 23 and Claudius 57. Pupils could be asked if this fact affects the way we view Messalina's behaviour. Does it also help to explain Claudius' indulgence towards her?

The story contains many examples of applied psychology. Messalina has the measure of everyone in her life, with the possible exception of Narcissus, whose ability to manipulate others is at least equal to hers. She loses the battle because Narcissus has access to Claudius and to the Praetorian Guard, with the result that she can only react to events, whereas he initiates them. His skill and speed of thought in handling people are remarkable; he stage-manages the downfall of Messalina with supreme efficiency. Pupils might be asked why Narcissus comes out on top while Messalina loses, and whether Claudius is a winner or loser in all this.

An excellent resource for further discussion is Robert Graves' *Claudius the God*, Chapters 28-9, and the BBC video based on the book.

avunculus meus

A day in the life of Pliny the Elder (Extracts from Pliny, *Letters* III.5.9-16)

These notes owe much to A.N.Sherwin-White, *The Letters of Pliny: A Historical and Social Commentary* (OUP).

Baebius Macer was *cōnsul suffectus* in AD 103 and was *praefectus urbis* in AD 117. This is the only letter addressed to him, and his relationship with Pliny is unclear.

- 1 **Vespasiānum imperātōrem:** he reigned from AD 69-79, and so Pliny is writing only of the last ten years of his uncle's life. The pre-dawn visit to the emperor was the *salūtātiō* paid by his *amīcī*, possibly followed by an advisory *cōnsilium*.
- 2-3 **officium...dēlēgātum:** this was the prefecture of the fleet at Misenum.
- 3 **domum:** although the elder Pliny had a house at Misenum, he appears to have administered the fleet mainly from an office in Rome.
- 4 **cibum:** this would be the *ientāculum,* a light breakfast.
- 5-6 **liber legēbātur:** i.e. by an educated slave. The notes and extracts would be made by another slave.
- 7 **excerperet:** generic subjunctive; such note-taking from the works of other writers was quite normal at this time (cf. VI.20.5, where the younger Pliny continued to make such extracts during the eruption of Vesuvius).
- 9 **gustābat:** the *gustātiō* or *prandium* was usually taken before bathing, but Pliny was in the habit of bathing first (cf. VI.16.5).
- 10 **dormiēbat:** the midday siesta was generally taken about the seventh hour.

    aliō diē: this is evidence that the standard working day for men of Pliny's class was over by midday. Pliny's 'second day' would have lasted from the seventh or eighth to the ninth hour.
- 14 **sōlum balineī tempus:** the genitive is adjectival, like a genitive of definition: 'only the time for bathing'.

    studiīs: dative of disadvantage: 'from his studies'.
- 15 **interiōribus:** i.e. the place of his actual immersion in the bath.

dēstringitur: this refers to the use of the strigil.

17-18 librō et pugillāribus: the secretary's task was both to read aloud and to take notes, since there was no room for another slave (see 6 above).

20 sellā: this was like a sedan chair and was used by Pliny because wheeled carriages were banned from the streets of Rome for most of the day.

21 poterās: 'you could have'. Potentiality resides in the verb itself and is therefore regularly expressed by the indicative.

Discussion

This letter gives a brief but graphic description of the elder Pliny's daily routine, which for him was subservient to literary activity, whether reading, note-taking or composing. His works cover a huge range of subjects, all of which are lost except for his main work, the thirty-seven books of the *Naturalis Historia*. Such closely focused energy can be seen also in the younger Pliny, several of whose letters testify to his own pervasive literary interests (e.g. I.6 and I.9); since the elder Pliny took an active interest in the education of his nephew (VI.16.7), perhaps this is not surprising. The letter also enables us to see beyond the uncle to the daily routine of the upper classes, for whom official work occupied a surprisingly small proportion of their time. Pupils may be able to suggest examples of other groups or individuals whose life is similarly dominated by a single obsession (such as international athletes, superstars in the performing arts). Is such an unbalanced life to be criticised or admired?

The death of Pliny the Elder (Extracts from Pliny, *Letters* VI.16.1, 4-20)

Tacitus received eleven letters from the younger Pliny, on a variety of topics, though literary, political and forensic themes predominate; this is hardly surprising, because they were contemporaries and pursued closely parallel careers and literary interests. The closeness (or otherwise) of their friendship has been the subject of much debate.

3 classem: the elder Pliny was in command of one of the two *classēs praetōriae* (Imperial standing fleets), which were stationed at

Ravenna and Misenum. The *praefectus* of the fleet nominally exercised *imperium* on behalf of the emperor, but in practice would probably have referred serious problems to Rome.

praesēns: in contrast with line 3 of the previous letter, Pliny was actually present at Misenum at the time of the eruption.

4 **hōrā ferē septimā:** i.e. between 2 and 3 p.m.

5 **nūbem mīrābilem:** the first stage of the eruption would involve the expulsion of the plug of solidified magma which had blocked the pipe or conduit connecting the cone with the magma chamber deep below the volcano. Pressure had built up over the centuries since the previous eruption until it overcame the resistance of the plug; this allowed the combination of superheated steam, gases and solid matter to shoot high into the stratosphere, giving rise to the cloud.

9 **cōdicillōs:** if this message arrived by sea, as appears most likely in view of Pliny's following comment, then why did Rectina not escape at the same time? Pliny himself expresses no surprise at this, and we must suppose that the boat bringing the letter was too small to accommodate Rectina and her personal slaves, together perhaps with valued possessions.

Tascī: Rectina was the wife of Tascius, probably the Pomponianus referred to in 24, who was at Stabiae. Presumably Rectina's house was near the coast further north near Herculaneum, and so more immediately threatened by the volcano.

13 **quadrirēmēs:** these were large warships with four banks of oars, capable of rescuing a large number of people, unlike the *liburnica* which he had originally intended to use for his own observations.

15 **festīnat illūc unde...fugiunt:** the chiastic word order neatly reflects the physical relationship of the two activities.

18 **dictāret adnotāretque:** the elder Pliny's scholarly habits (cf. 6 and 11 of the previous letter) persist even in the midst of danger.

19-21 **iam...iam...iam:** the repetition of *iam*, together with the use of comparative adjectives, indicates the progressive deterioration of the situation.

21 **vadum subitum:** the sea bed has risen, effectively moving the

coastline further away from Herculaneum.
21-2 **ruīnā...obstantia:** 'the shore blocked their way with debris from the mountain': the falling ash and mud flows also pushed the coastline out to sea.
23-4 **fortēs...fortūna adiuvat:** quoted from Terence, *Phormio* 203 (cf. Virgil, *Aeneid* X.284: *audentēs fortūna iuvat*).
25 **sinū mediō:** it is unclear whether Pliny is referring to the Bay of Naples itself or the smaller extension of the bay which has Oplontis at its northern and Stabiae at its southern end, with Pompeii in the middle. Since Pliny assumes Tacitus to be familiar with the general topography, it seems unlikely that he would give such a description of the whole bay, because Tacitus would have needed a description of only the less familiar local features. It is the more difficult for us to decide now because of extensive changes in the shore-line in the vicinity of Pompeii, which before the eruption was by the sea.
36 **in remedium formīdinis:** 'to allay the fears' (of those around him). **ignēs:** bonfires would be a common sight on farmland. Pliny of course was telling a brave lie to comfort the rest.
37 **agrestium:** because of the fertility of the volcanic soil, the slopes of Vesuvius were extensively cultivated by farmers living in the *vīllae*.
40 **gravior et sonantior:** 'rather heavy and noisy'. The force of the comparatives is 'more...than average'.
40-1 **eīs quī līminī obversābantur:** either personal slaves or anyone else in the house (since we are told in 44-5 that everyone else stayed awake).
41-3 **ārea...surrēxerat:** i.e. the level of the courtyard had risen.
42 **cinere mixtīsque pūmicibus:** notice how the sense of *mixtīs* has dictated the elegant word order: the two nouns enclose the participle that binds them together.
51-2 **apud illum...vīcit:** Pliny uses an elegant and chiastic phrase to express the contrast between his uncle's sang-froid and the panic of everyone else: he weighed up the rational arguments, while they were swayed by the greater terror.
54 **alibī, illīc:** note the antithesis.

55 facēs…lūmina: Pliny further enhances his vivid narrative with another chiasmus.

60-1 aliōs…illum: another chiasmus to highlight the contrast between Pliny and his companions.

65-6 diēs…tertius: by our reckoning, this would be the second day after the last daylight seen by the elder Pliny (the Romans counted the day at both ends of the sequence), i.e. 26 August. The sequence of events was as follows:

24 August: the eruption begins and the elder Pliny sails to Stabiae in daylight.

25 August: daylight disappears and he dies (the others presumably escape).

26 August: his body is found.

67 opertum…indūtus: it is unclear whether Pliny is trying to show that his uncle was not *murdered* by his slaves or just that he died peacefully.

Discussion

This is the first of two letters in which Pliny describes the eruption of Vesuvius; in the second one (VI.20), a response to a further request from Tacitus, he describes the effects of the eruption as he himself experienced them at Misenum. When reading VI.16, we have to remember that Tacitus has asked Pliny for an account of his uncle's death rather than of the actual eruption; it is inevitable, therefore, that we should feel only partly satisfied by a description which leaves many questions unanswered. Archaeology has been able to fill in some of the gaps, and conversely Pliny confirms the archaeological record in respect of the direction of the wind, the ash-fall and the alteration of the coastline. We are left wondering how the message from Rectina reached Pliny against the direction of the wind, whether Pliny's warships succeeded in rescuing any of the inhabitants of Stabiae or whether there were other fatalities besides Pliny, and what happened to Rectina and people living in or near Herculaneum. Some light has been shed on this last question by the recent discovery of human skeletons in caves by the harbour of Herculaneum: one or more family groups were trapped by the rising tide of mud as they waited in vain for rescue by sea.

The letter may be explored from several angles. It is of undoubted historical value for its clear, factual account of the eruption; it provides an interesting character sketch of the elder Pliny; and we glimpse something of the younger Pliny's own personality through his obvious admiration for his uncle and his economical but vivid description of the stages of the eruption.

A reconstruction of the events and interpretation of the details are valuable activities for the pupil. The notes on 9 and 65-6, the change of plan at 11-12 and the fateful decision at 24, may help to fuel discussion.

It is worth remembering that both letters were written more than twenty years after the events described in them, which raises the question of the accuracy of Pliny's memory: he was only seventeen at the time of his uncle's death, but his observations are those of a more mature mind. Did he make detailed notes, following the example of his uncle?

sāgae Thessalae
(Extracts from Apuleius, *Metamorphoses* II.21-30)

The *Metamorphoses*, better known as 'The Golden Ass', written probably in the second half of the second century AD, is the only complete Roman novel to survive (the *Satyrica* of Petronius is incomplete). It follows the adventures of Lucius, whose curiosity about witchcraft led to his metamorphosis into an ass. The present episode takes place before his transformation. The language is essentially simple, despite the frequent use of words and expressions which were rare in the first century.

1 **iuvenis:** 'when a young man'.

Mīlētō profectus: Miletus is chosen because the city gave its name to a type of story, well-known among the Greeks and Romans, which took the form of an entertaining anecdote of a rather risqué kind. Apuleius actually begins his *Metamorphoses* with a declaration that his tale is to be 'in the Milesian mode'.

2 **haec etiam loca prōvinciae:** i.e. Thelyphron wanted to visit Thessaly as well as Olympia.

3 **peragrātā tōtā Thessaliā:** the placing of the participle at the beginning of the phrase is a regular feature of Apuleius' style.

4 **tenuātō viāticō:** ablative absolute.

5 **īnsistēbat lapidem:** Apuleius frequently treats such compound verbs as transitive (cf. *accēdēns senem* (21-2) and *cadāver accurrō* (41)).

6 **mortuum custōdīre:** 'to guard a dead man'. The guarding of a tomb after burial was a common practice in the Roman period, but this is the only known reference to the guarding of a body before burial. It is unknown whether Apuleius invented the idea or whether it was a practice peculiar to Thessaly. Thelyphron's sarcastic comment '*hīc...aufugere?*' in 8-9 suggests that the custom was unusual.

10 **puer:** used derogatively, to mean 'stupid'.

11 **sāgae:** Thessaly was renowned in antiquity for its witchcraft. Indeed, this tradition may be traced back to the presence there of Medea, who settled at Iolcus with Jason after his return with the

Golden Fleece. Lucan (*Pharsalia* VI. 435-569) gives a lurid account of Thessalian witchcraft, including the practice of biting off the tongue of an unburied corpse.

21 **animum meum commasculō:** *lit.* 'I make my mind manly'. Perhaps a pun is intended here, since the name Thelyphron means 'with a woman's mind'. Here and in the following line, he presents a manly figure, but by the end of his story, all his courage has evaporated.

23 **vix finieram et:** a colloquialism, like the English 'I had scarcely finished and...'.

24 **fuscis vestimentis:** note the precise detail; the Thessalians, like other Greeks, would wear black for mourning, whereas the Romans normally wore white.

26 **splendentibus...coopertum:** the wrapping of the body in white sheets was a normal part of the *prothesis*, the period of a day between death and the funeral when the body was laid on a couch in a room of the house. Since death was a pollution, the body had to be purified and white, the colour associated with purity, was the natural choice. Poor people were covered with rags.

27 **ubi...dēmōnstrāvit:** the widow wished Thelyphron to witness that nose, ears, eyes, lips and chin were still intact before he began his vigil.

29-30 **dum animum...cantātiōnibus:** note that the singing was not to keep him awake, but to soothe him: his courage was already wavering.

31-2 **cum...cōnstitit:** the 'inverse' *cum* takes the indicative.

32 **mustēla:** in the classical world the weasel was the familiar of witches, a sinister creature that brought bad luck.

37-8 **deus...Delphicus:** so alike were they that not even Apollo, with his power of prophecy, could distinguish the living from the dead.

46 **istīus fēminae:** we are to visualise the old man pointing an accusing finger at the supposedly mourning widow.

49 **ob praedam hērēditāriam:** 'to steal the inheritance'. There was a long tradition, at least in literature, of wives poisoning their husbands to get their hands on their wealth.

53 **Zatchlas:** the origin of this name is unknown: it is not Egyptian. It is possibly an error in the transcription of the text by a scribe.

90 Commentary: prose selections

Aegyptius: Egypt had long been associated with the practice of mystical and magical arts, especially in relation to death and the progress of the soul after death. What Thelyphron fails to tell us is why Zatchlas was so conveniently available. It is possible that he was associated with a local cult of Isis.

58-60 tumōre...cadāver: in *Pharsalia* VI. lines 750ff., Lucan describes a Thessalian witch raising a shade from the dead: 'the clotted blood grew warm and coursed into the veins and extremities of the limbs. The organs trembled in the cold breast. Next all his limbs quivered. The man rose upright at once.'

extollī...implērī: the historic infinitives may need explanation.

60, 61 Lēthaea, Stygiīs: these names must be intended to impress the audience, since, if the soul of the corpse had drunk from Lethe, it would have been unable to recall the circumstances of its death. The traditional view was that a soul drank from Lethe before reincarnation.

61 Stygiīs palūdibus: although the Styx was conventionally represented as the river encircling the Underworld, it was sometimes represented as a lake or marsh (cf. Virgil, *Aeneid* VI.323: *Cōcȳtī stāgna alta vidēs Stygiamque palūdem*: 'You see the deep pools of Cocytus and the marsh of Styx.').

62 redūcitis, dēsine: the change from plural to singular indicates that the corpse turns from the crowd to the prophet.

65 commōtior: the context does not make it clear whether the prophet is speaking more forcefully than the corpse, or than he himself had done previously (even though no previous words have been quoted).

quīn nārrās?: the tone is more peremptory than that conveyed by the literal translation 'why don't you tell?'

68 novae nūptae: this confirms the old man's accusation in 49 that the murderess was a legacy-hunter.

69 tepentem: the husband's death had barely given time for the bed to cool before the widow invited her lover into it.

70-1 documenta vēritātis...indicābō: in fact the corpse gives no proof of his wife's guilt, only of Thelyphron's mutilation.

71 **cognōverit, ōmināverit:** perfect subjunctive to express a generic idea. Translate 'could know or predict'.

73,75 **sagācissimus exsertam vigiliam, industriam sēdulam:** it is arguable whether these words are sincere or ironic.

77 **sepelīvērunt:** an appropriate metaphor, in view of Thelyphron's description in 36-9.

78-9 **hebetēs...frīgida:** note the chiasmus.

79-80 **ad artis magicae obsequia...nītuntur:** 'struggle to obey the commands of their magic art'.

80-1 **tantum sopōre mortuus:** 'only dead asleep', *lit.* 'only dead from sleep'.

81 **idem mēcum nōmen...habet:** the identity of names is a vital element of the story.

84-5 **per quoddam forāmen:** because the door was locked, the witches reach in through a hole in the door. In translation it may help to expand the phrase: 'the witches reached in through a hole and cut off...'.

92-3 **inter pedēs...effugiō:** this suggests that Thelyphron escaped on all fours.

96 **linteolō istō:** Thelyphron points to a small piece of cloth which all the time has been covering the part of his face where his nose should have been.

Discussion

Some scholars have argued that this episode is in fact a composite of three separate stories: the first is the story of a man hired to watch over a corpse; the second tells of the scheming of the witches to obtain pieces of flesh; the third is a sequel involving necromancy and adultery to make the composite more colourful.

Alternatively, the episode might be seen as a conflation of two stories: in the first, a man guards a corpse but, because he has the same name as the corpse, he becomes the witches' victim instead of the corpse; in the second, a corpse is temporarily brought back from the dead to denounce his murderer. Pupils could be asked whether they think the combination of the stories is successful or whether they would be better kept separate. They may like the way the first story (or stories) is kept unresolved until the last story has been told. Against this, it can be argued that Apuleius is clumsy when he leaves this last story hanging in the air - we are not told what happened to the widow in the face of the corpse's accusations, because the corpse switches to the Thelyphron story.

The story is full of unexpected twists and turns and teachers will need to check that pupils understand what is going on. One entertaining way of doing this is for the teacher to stop at various critical points, revise what has happened and then ask the class to guess what happens next before finding out what actually occurs. A likely difficulty for pupils is that the details of the events recounted by the corpse, especially in 77-86, are not fully explained. The reader has to read between the lines to deduce that the witches can get a victim into their power only if they call him by name or perhaps that they can mutilate him only if they can gain access to his body - hence their need to bring Thelyphron to the hole in the door. There are also inconsistencies: it is hard to believe that Thelyphron would not have noticed his mutilations until the corpse mentioned them.

Pupils could also be asked to list the elements in the story which are calculated to keep the reader interested, such as the spooky (nocturnal watch over corpse, appearance of weasel); the macabre (mutilation); magic (witches, Zatchlas, resurrection of corpse); sex (adultery of wife); the surprise of the two Thelyphrons and the mutilation of the wrong one.

The characters are shallow - even Thelyphron himself is little more than a vehicle for the telling of the story. It is the fast-moving plot, however, crammed with events, which rewards the reader.

Although it is difficult to sustain an argument that Apuleius is warning the reader against meddling in witchcraft, pupils may like to discuss the possibility. More persuasive, perhaps, is his own exhortation at the beginning of the work: *lēctor intende: laetāberis* 'pay attention, reader, and you will be delighted'. This does indeed seem to be his purpose, at least in this episode. A subtle humour at work is suggested by the plays on the name Thelyphron, by little flourishes like the comparison between the two Thelyphrons (36-9), and by the living Thelyphron's reactions to the corpse's revelations. Note also the contrast between the confident young traveller at the beginning of the story and the broken man at the end.

trēs fēminae

Arria (Extracts from Pliny, Letters III.16)

These notes owe much to A.N.Sherwin-White, *The Letters of Pliny: A Historical and Social Commentary* (OUP). Nepos was either Maecilius or Metilius Nepos, a literary senator, who received three other letters from Pliny: II.3, IV.26 and VI.19.

1 **Caecina Paetus:** he was *consul suffectus* in AD 37 before becoming involved in the revolt of 42.
2 **fīlius:** we do not know the name of this son.
4 **fūnus...exsequiās:** note the chiastic word order.
5 **quotiēns...intrāret:** the use of the subjunctive after *quotiēns* is confined to Livy and Silver Age writers.
7 **quid ageret** (cf. the common phrase *quid agis?* 'how are you?').
13 **illud factum:** pupils will need to be told that Pliny is leaping ahead to the climax of the famous story before giving the less well-known preliminaries.
15-16 **Paete, nōn dolet:** Martial relates a variant of these words of Arria:
'sī qua fidēs, vulnus quod fēcī nōn dolet,' inquit,
    'sed tū quod faciēs, hoc mihi, Paete, dolet.' (*Epigrams* I.13).
17 **Scrībōniānus:** L.Arruntius Camillus Scribonianus had been consul in AD 32 and in 42 was legate of Dalmatia in control of two legions. The revolt against Claudius began in Rome among a group of equites and senators; when Scribonianus became involved, Caecina Paetus and his wife must have been with him. The conspiracy lasted fifteen days, and when the legions refused to join in, Scribonianus was forced to flee and either took his own life or was killed by a soldier. See also Suetonius, *Claudius* 13.
20 **cōnsulārī virō:** see note on 1.
21 **quōrum ē manū cibum capiat:** it was customary for slaves of wealthy households to cut up food into small enough pieces to enable diners to eat without the need for cutlery. Arria's request would not therefore appear extravagant. Arria assumes that her husband is innocent until proved guilty, and so is still entitled to the

privileges of an ex-consul.

- **25 apud Claudium:** the trial of Paetus was held before the senate in the presence of the emperor.
  uxōrī Scrībōniānī: her name was Vibia.
- **26-7 egone...vīvis:** Arria contrasts her own bravery and loyalty to her husband with the twofold betrayal of her husband by Vibia: not only did she not take her own life when he died, but she was now betraying his memory by turning informer.
- **28-9 cōnsilium...fuisse:** Arria was already intending suicide, here considered a 'glorious death'.
- **29 Thrasea:** P.Clodius Thrasea Paetus was married to Arria's daughter, the younger Arria, who in turn was the mother of Fannia who recounted these stories to Pliny.
- **31 filiam tuam:** the younger Arria. Thrasea is contemplating a situation which actually occurred in AD 66, when the younger Arria wished to follow her mother's example, but was persuaded by her husband to live for the sake of their daughter.
- **35 male moriar:** i.e. slowly and painfully.
- **36 adversō:** note the common idiomatic sense 'full tilt', 'head on'.

Discussion

Pliny sets out in this letter to argue that Arria's most famous act, her suicide with the words *Paete, nōn dolet,* was not her greatest act. He claims that two other examples of her courage (the concealment of the death of her son and her self-destructive determination to die with her husband) were even more remarkable. Although the passages in which Pliny presents this argument have been omitted here, it is still worthwhile to compare the heroism of the three acts.

Pupils could well discuss why the story of Arria's suicide was so immensely popular in antiquity. Is it because such selfless devotion was rare in Roman society and so had the value of novelty? Or is she the model of the ideal wife (at least in the eyes of a largely male-dominated literary community)? Another approach is to compare ancient and modern views about suicide: would Arria's self-sacrifice evoke as much praise today? Pupils might also be asked which of Arria's deeds they find most touching.

Do they find her actions too theatrical to evoke sympathy?

Calpurnia (Pliny, *Letters* IV.19)

Calpurnia was Pliny's third wife and little more than a girl when he married her. Hispulla's family, like Pliny's, came from Comum in northern Italy; her brother, Calpurnia's father, had died some time previously.

- 2 **amantissimum tuī:** objective genitive (cf. *amōrem meī* (9)).
  parī amōre: i.e. with a love equal to his love for her.
- 10 **āctūrus:** Carcopino, *Daily Life in Ancient Rome* (Penguin) pp.208ff., has a vivid description of the Court of the Centumviri, where Pliny often spoke. Carcopino conveys very clearly the showbusiness element of Roman lawcourts implied by Pliny in 11-12.
- 14-15 **versūs...meōs:** Pliny had a life-long interest in composing poetry (cf. VII.4, where he describes the variety of metre he has attempted and the degree of success his verses have achieved).
- 15 **cantat...citharā** (cf. VII.4 where he says that his verses were 'sung and set to music for the lyre even by Greeks persuaded to learn Latin by love of my little book').
- 21 **tuīs manibus ēdūcātam:** Calpurnia's mother must have died when Calpurnia was very young.
- 24 **mātrem meam:** this was Plinia, sister of Pliny the Elder. This friendship probably accounts for the marriage.

Discussion

This letter is useful for the insight it gives into the relationship of Pliny with his young wife. The marriage appears to have been arranged through family contact and Calpurnia's love for Pliny seems to have grown with time; whether Pliny genuinely loved his wife is difficult to judge, but he certainly appreciated her intellectual qualities, as she did his. Despite the letter's condescending and self-congratulatory tone, the last sentence suggests an equal partnership surprising for Roman times. (Another apparently exceptional marriage was that of Turia and her unnamed husband; see *Turia* in the *Cambridge Latin Course* Unit IVB, Stage 43.) Pupils could be asked to probe the reasons for Pliny's optimism in 17-18. He and

Calpurnia apparently share interests in literature and music, but she does not yet participate fully in the society of Pliny's literary friends, from either shyness or social convention.

Pupils might also consider whether arranged marriages such as this one are a good idea, especially when there is such a disparity in age. What might be the advantages of the marriage for Pliny and Calpurnia? Teachers might read a translation of VI.4 and 7 which seem to show the growing mutual affection of the couple.

As for Hispulla, this letter contains almost as much praise for her as for the young Calpurnia. Her qualities *in locō parentis* compare well with those of Ummidia in the next letter.

Ummidia Quadrātilla (Extracts from Pliny, *Letters* VII.24)

This letter is conceptually and linguistically difficult and pupils will need considerable help to understand both the surface meaning and the underlying ideas. Rosianus Geminus was Pliny's consular quaestor in AD 100.

- 1 **Ummidia Quadrātilla:** she was born in about AD 26, giving a probable date for this letter of about AD 104-5.
- 1-2 **paulō minus octōgēnsimō...annō:** she was probably about seventy-eight.
- 3-4 **ultrā mātrōnālem modum:** i.e. in view of the hazards of childbirth.
- 5 **testāmentum...optimum:** it was excellent because she left the bulk of her property to her grandchildren and gave virtually nothing to the sycophantic individuals mentioned in 27ff.
  hērēdēs: 'as her heirs'.
- 5-6 **ex besse, ex tertiā parte:** the meaning of these legal terms is clear enough: the grandson would receive two-thirds of the estate and the granddaughter one-third.
- 6 **neptem vix nōvī:** this suggests that Pliny was not a close family friend.
- 7 **nepōtem:** this is the young Ummidius Quadratus, whose honesty and eloquence Pliny praises in VI.11. Little is known of him except that he enjoyed political success under Hadrian.
- 8-9 **etiam eī quōs...amant:** the meaning of this difficult clause is, 'even

those to whom he is not related love him as if he were'.
11 **intrā quārtum et vīcēnsimum annum:** such an early marriage was not unusual for men of his class. Had he still been unmarried at 25 he would have been precluded by the *lēx Iūlia* from inheriting a legacy.
13 **dēlicātam sevĕrissimē:** note the antithesis. Pliny is trying to show the contrast not only between the characters of Ummidia and Quadratus, but also between Ummidia's personal tastes and her sense of responsibility towards her grandson.
14 **pantomīmōs:** the pantomimus was an actor who combined the roles of tragic actor, opera singer and ballet dancer and who would be accompanied by musicians and chorus; here the plural refers to the whole troupe. Although Tiberius had passed a law restraining senators and equites from associating openly with them and public performances by them had been banned by Domitian and Trajan, it seems these laws quickly lapsed. Ummidia's possession of a private troupe of actors is criticised by Pliny (a) explicitly, on the grounds that she wasted too much money on them; (b) implicitly, perhaps, on the grounds that pantomime actors were disreputable and even immoral (both in their performances and in their private lives).
17 **studia:** Pliny was entrusted with Quadratus' entry into the legal profession.
18 **in illō ōtiō sexūs:** women of high birth and wealth had little to occupy them, because they were denied a public career and the abundance of slaves left them few domestic responsibilities.
lūsū calculōrum: gambling in public was proscribed by law.
21 **reverentiā:** perhaps Ummidia was sensitive to the law; Pliny, however, is again praising her sense of responsibility to her grandson. There is also a paradox: *reverentia* is usually an attitude adopted by young people towards the old; here the old lady shows *reverentia* to her young grandson.
23–4 **sacerdōtālibus lūdīs:** although *lūdī* more often meant chariot races or gladiatorial contests, it is clear from the context that Pliny is here referring to drama competitions.

26 **hodiē prīmum:** these two words should be taken together.

27 **aliēnissimī hominēs:** note the contrast achieved by placing these words next to *nepōs*. Pliny does not make it clear whether these were applauders actually hired for the purpose by Ummidia (cf. II.14, where he calls them *laudicēnī*) or whether they were *clientēs* or just freelances. If they were *clientēs* or *lībertī* of Ummidia, Pliny's *aliēnissimī* would be rhetorical exaggeration.

28 **pudet mē dīxisse honōrem:** Pliny rightly observes that fawning attention is not indicative of respect.

30 **singulōs gestūs...reddēbant:** i.e. whenever Ummidia applauded or gesticulated, so did her fan-club.

cum canticīs: perhaps they joined in the singing which accompanied the dances.

31 **minima lēgāta:** perhaps the main motivation for these applauders was the expectation of a bequest (cf. Regulus in **persōnae nōn grātae**). Ummidia's minimal acknowledgement of them in her will shows that she was impervious to their attentions. There is a degree of irony in the last sentence because their hopes of success, already only modest, were further reduced by Ummidia's discouragement of Quadratus from associating with her indulgences.

Discussion

Pliny's praise of Ummidia is balanced by criticism of her extravagant tastes, partly expressed through his admiration for the successful avoidance of exposure to these excesses by Quadratus. The qualities in Ummidia that Pliny finds praiseworthy are her common-sense and her proper sense of responsibility for the upbringing of Quadratus, whose self-control, modesty and obedience he equally admires.

Pupils may initially see Ummidia as a hypocritical killjoy, telling her grandson (a man in his twenties), 'Do as I say, not as I do'. How would he have felt as an adolescent, being forever sent out of the room when entertainment appeared? Sherwin-White, however, points out that Ummidia herself had been young in the reign of Nero, when frivolity, gambling and theatre-going took precedence over serious pursuits for some aristocrats, but that times had changed by Pliny's day: society had become stricter, and law and government demanded more commitment. Ummidia, therefore, may have felt that if Quadratus wanted a public career, his style of life would have to be very different from her own.

Pupils may like to consider whether society today is in a similar periodic swing between licence and puritanism. They could also discuss their reactions to the attitudes of Ummidia, Quadratus and Pliny.

persōnae nōn grātae

Pȳthius (Cicero, De Officiis III.58)

The *De Officiis* sets out to establish appropriate action to be taken in a variety of circumstances calling for moral judgement. Cicero's response generally follows the Stoic principle that moral goodness is the only real good and so outweighs all other considerations.

- 2-3 **quō...ubi...posset:** the subjunctive expresses purpose.
- 7 **hominem:** 'him', i.e. Canius; but it is also possible that the use of the word sounds a note of contempt.
- 9-10 **dīxit...quid...vellet:** i.e. their instructions for producing fish on cue. Pupils might be helped to appreciate the skill with which Cicero tells the story if they are asked why he does not say at this point what the instructions were.
- 12 **pedēs Pȳthiī piscēs:** note the alliteration; similarly in 15 and indeed throughout the passage. It adds to the raciness and humour of the piece.
- 22 **quid faceret?:** a deliberative question.

Discussion

This is a straightforward passage requiring little contextual detail, since the story is self-contained. It is a confidence-trick of timeless inspiration, a trap perfectly sprung, in which the con-man snares his victim through the latter's greed. However, when introducing class discussion it is worth keeping in mind Cicero's purpose in relating the story. Pupils may like to consider to what extent Pythius has broken any law and whether anyone can be morally justified in pursuing his own interest at the expense of someone else's. Does Canius contribute at all to his own misfortune? And if Canius is at fault, to what extent (if any) does this excuse Pythius? Cicero's language repays attention: in contrast with his speeches, his expression here is economical and factual with little comment or judgement: he lets the events speak for themselves. Thus a rapid pace is maintained, helped perhaps by the remarkable amount of alliteration of 'p's and 'c's, focused on the names of the two principal characters; also the

personae non gratae 101

sentences are short and verbs often omitted.
Pupils might consider why the implied answer to the question at the end is so negative. Cicero goes on to explain that legislation on criminal fraud had not yet come into force. Teachers might introduce pupils to the phrase *caveat emptor* and discuss with them different kinds of fraudulent behaviour, e.g. *suppressio veri* and *suggestio falsi*.

Rēgulus (Extract from Pliny, *Letters* II.20)

M. Aquilius Regulus is the subject of several letters (I.5; IV.2, 7; VI.2). Whilst Pliny admired his advocacy in the civil courts, he despised his politically-motivated prosecutions and personal morality.

1 **assem parā**: Pliny pretends to be offering his stories for sale, like a professional story-teller.

  auream: this may be rendered as 'splendid', but its literal meaning of 'golden' provides a neat contrast with *assem*, the lowest denomination of coin, made of copper. Note the chiastic arrangement of *assem...auream* which heightens the contrasts between the four words.

3 **Vērānia**: the wife of L. Calpurnius Piso, who was murdered in AD 69 by the supporters of Otho. At the time of the incident recounted here, she was very old.

4 **impudentiam**: exclamatory accusative. 'Look at the impudence of the man!'

4-5 **marītō...invīsissimus**: Regulus was said to have savaged the severed head of the murdered Piso.

5 **sī vēnit tantum**: 'if he had done no more than pay her a visit'.

6-7 **quō diē...interrogāvit**: to work out her horoscope; Regulus' superstition was well-known.

7-8 **compōnit vultum...movet labra**: signs of concentration.

8 **agitat digitōs**: the Romans regularly used their fingers for counting.
  nihil: i.e. he made no reply.

9-10 **clīmactēricum tempus**: ancient astrologers reckoned that critical points occurred every seventh year of life.

10-11 **haruspicem cōnsulam**: since consulting astrologers was forbidden by law, Regulus was forced to content himself with the officially approved soothsayers, who foretold the future by examining the entrails of sacrificed animals.

13 **ut in perīculō crēdula:** 'inclined to believe him because she felt herself in danger'.

15-16 **plūs etiam quam periūrum:** 'worse even than an oath-breaker': the Romans believed that perjury was the worst form of deceit, and the next phrase explains why this particular perjury was particularly despicable.

16 **quī sibi...pēierāvisset:** 'who had sworn a false oath on the welfare of his son'. Swearing by the life or welfare of a close relative was a standard form of oath in Rome.

16-17 **facit hoc...frequenter:** i.e. his practice was as frequent as it was wicked.

18-19 **in caput...dētestātur:** because of the oath, Regulus deflects divine punishment for his perjury from himself to his son. The son died about five years later (*Letters* IV.2).

20 **Vellēius Blaesus:** little is known of him, beyond a mention of his death in about AD 93 by Martial (VIII.38).

23 **captāre:** in its neutral sense, this means no more than the cultivation of friendship; in its pejorative sense, it implies legacy-hunting.

hortārī et rogāre: the historic infinitives may need to be explained.

Discussion

Pupils might consider the different ways in which, according to Pliny, Regulus transgressed the unwritten canon of acceptable behaviour. Does Pliny condemn him for visiting Verania because she was sick? Certainly he sees it as a mark of impudence that he visited her at all (doubtless because of the way he had revelled in her husband's death and prosecuted her brother-in-law). Why did Regulus tell Verania that she would survive the critical moment? Why did she feel threatened if he reassured her that the entrails accorded with the stars? Why did she alter her will to benefit Regulus? Part of the answer to these questions is that Regulus made her believe that her main hope of surviving the crisis rested upon his astrological skill. Her subsequent decline proved him false and her reliance upon him misplaced, but too late to change her will again. This interpretation is not spelt out by Pliny: we condemn him by inference and because of Verania's words. Does this mean that Pliny was reluctant to accuse him explicitly in case he incurred a charge of calumny?

A second point for discussion is the practice of *captātiō* or legacy-hunting. The cultivation of wealthy people by juniors and social inferiors was usual in Roman society, and was actively encouraged through the system of patronage; it was also usual for such protégés to expect some reward in the form of a bequest; indeed, society placed a moral obligation to include in one's will all with a claim to *amīcitia*. Such a system was, however, open to abuse: it was all too likely that unscrupulous men would make the bequest, rather than social advancement, their principal aim, and target the gullible or the fragile. Verania was an ideal target, because she was old, childless, widowed and ailing. Regulus needed no social advancement, being motivated purely by greed.

Pupils could be asked about the differences between the two stories. The story of Blaesus is not told in such an interesting way nor with such a strong sense of indignation - its point is in the twist at the end.

Semprōnia (Sallust, *Catilina* 25)

After his electoral defeat in June 64 BC, Catiline gathered whatever support he could find to fuel his planned rebellion. Inevitably those who flocked to his banner were the ones with most to gain from the disruption of the economic and political system; among these were debtors, including women who had funded extravagant life-styles by means of prostitution while they were young enough, and then had run up enormous debts; their hope was for the cancellation of debts promised by Catiline.

   1 **in eīs:** i.e. among the women who supported Catiline.
      Semprōnia: she was a member of the illustrious family of the Sempronii.
   2 **marītō:** her husband was D. Iunius Brutus, consul in 77 BC.
   3 **līberīs:** she was probably the mother of Decimus Brutus, one of the assassins of Julius Caesar.

satis fortūnāta: i.e. fortunate enough not to need to step outside the bounds of propriety.

3-4 **litterīs...docta:** such a high standard of education was unusual for a woman.

4 **ēlegantius quam necesse est:** Sempronia overstepped the limits of proficiency considered acceptable for a Roman *mātrōna*. Her accomplishments were associated with women of the *demi-monde* who belonged to a tradition going back to the great courtesans of Athens.

5 **multa...alia facere:** i.e. she had many other accomplishments which were put to improper use.

7 **discernerēs:** potential subjunctive.

10 **fidem prōdiderat:** 'she had broken her word'.

13-14 **multae facētiae...inerat:** 'she possessed a great deal of wit and charm'.

Discussion

This episode forms a digression from the main account of the conspiracy, exemplifying Sallust's interest in moral issues, especially in what he considered to be a general decline in moral standards within his own lifetime. One way to approach this is to try to establish what Sallust thought of as the ideal standard of matronly behaviour, and then judge the extent to which Sempronia deviated from this norm. Another way would be for pupils to draw up lists of her good and bad qualities. Do pupils share Sallust's disapproval of not only her involvement in murder and her untrustworthiness but also her other 'bad' qualities (e.g. her lyre-playing, extravagance and dancing)? Both of these approaches could generate fruitful comparisons with attitudes of today. One might also ask why Sallust thought it worthwhile to introduce a digression about Sempronia, who plays no further part in the action. One possible reason is Sallust's fascination with a remarkable woman who was both talented and intelligent and apparently morally degenerate.

Clōdia (Extracts from Cicero, *Pro Caelio* 34-6)

Cicero delivered his speech on 4 April, 56 BC. He began by defending Caelius' character and career against accusations of impropriety and treasonable activities (including complicity in the conspiracy of Catiline). After hinting that those who brought the prosecution against Caelius were not acting for themselves, he accused Clodia of being the source.

1 **ex nōbilī genere:** the *gēns Claudia* was one of the most ancient and illustrious of Rome.

   familiam clārissimam: Clodia had married her cousin, Q. Metellus Celer, consul in 60 BC. His sudden death in 59 led to rumours that Clodia, whose relationship with her husband was far from cordial, had poisoned him.

2 **tibi:** Clodia.

   coniūnctus: Caelius rented an apartment from Clodia's brother on the Palatine, which brought him into close proximity with Clodia, shortly after her husband's death, when she should have been in mourning.

4 **accūsātōrēs:** that is, those who are accusing Caelius. Cicero's point is that these accusations, although directed at Caelius, inevitably incriminate Clodia herself.

5 **Bāiās:** i.e. trips to Baiae; details of the dissolute life of Baiae may be found in Seneca, *Letters* 51.4,12.

   nāvigia: i.e. pleasure cruises at Baiae.

   iactant: i.e. against Caelius.

6 **affirmant...dīcere:** 'they acknowledge that they say nothing without your approval'; this suggests that Clodia herself was behind the charges against Caelius.

7-9 **aut refūtāre...testimōniō:** Cicero turns the tables neatly on Clodia here: either she must deny these allegations, in which case the case against Caelius collapses; or she must admit them, in which case her own character will be so blackened (because she was involved in the scandalous episodes just as much as Caelius) that she will become completely discredited in the eyes of the public: 'neither your accusation nor your evidence can be trusted'.

10 **vīcīnum:** the affair presumably began only after Caelius moved house.
12 **hortīs:** probably the gardens of Clodia's villa.
13 **parcī ac tenācis:** little is known of Caelius' father beyond the fact that he was an *eques*. The suggestion is that Clodia would have expected Caelius to be only too happy to compensate for his frugal upbringing. If his father still held the purse strings, a liaison with a rich woman could be an escape.
15 **cōnfer tē aliō:** i.e. try someone else.
15-17 **ēmistī hortōs...legās:** the argument is that Clodia has made herself readily available to young men of leisure, of whom she can (and probably does) have her pick; so why should she be so vindictive to Caelius?

Discussion

M. Caelius Rufus was almost certainly the Rufus attacked by Catullus in Poem 77, and probably supplanted Catullus in Clodia's affections. For further discussion of this see R.G.Austin, *Pro Caelio*, 3rd edition (OUP) Appendix III, pp.148-50. (A distinctly different view is argued forcefully by T.P.Wiseman, *Catullus and his world*, pp.15-53.)

The charge of attempted poisoning was one of five charges against Caelius, all of them probably instigated by Clodia in an attempt to ruin Caelius because he had broken off his two-year affair with her. To make the charge succeed, the prosecution had to blacken Caelius' character.

In this passage, Cicero first refutes the accusations against Caelius by discrediting their source, Clodia. Then he accuses Clodia of having ensnared Caelius amidst a more general pattern of promiscuity. The ridicule he heaps upon her was so effective that Clodia was soon laughed out of court, and Caelius was acquitted.

Pupils may wish to discuss the tone of this extract. How persuasive is Cicero? Does he give proof or merely accusation? Pupils could also be asked what lines 15-17 have to do with the poison charge: if they are irrelevant, why does Cicero include them? Is it in response to the prosecution's attempts to blacken Caelius' character? Would a modern-day judge allow any parts of this extract to be uttered in court?

A further topic of discussion is a comparison of Clodia with Sempronia: are there any similarities between them? Do the two writers approach their targets in similar ways? (For example, Sallust 9 may be compared with Cicero 15-17.)

108 Commentary: prose selections

Druidēs

Julius Caesar's account (Extracts from Caesar, *Gallic War* VI.13-16)

In the spring of 53 BC, Caesar doused the last embers of the revolt among the Gauls led by Ambiorix. The Germanic Treveri had briefly joined the revolt and called upon other Germanic tribes from across the Rhine to support them. To prevent such support, Caesar built a bridge and crossed the Rhine. Finding himself at the junction of Gallic and Germanic cultures, he decided that this would be an appropriate point in his narrative to describe 'the customs of Gaul and Germany' (*Gallic War* VI. 11). He begins his description with an analysis of the Gallic tribal groupings and proceeds to an account of the Druids and the knights, the two dominant social classes throughout Gaul. The Druids are the main religious, judicial and cultural force, the knights the military, political and administrative.

The power of the Druids

1 **pūblica ac prīvāta:** Caesar uses this distinction three times in this passage, but his meaning is not entirely clear. Here he refers to sacrifices on behalf of both the whole tribe and the individual tribesman. The distinction intended between *pūblicīs* and *prīvātīs* in 5 must be slightly different: either he is distinguishing disputes between tribes from disputes between individuals within the same tribe, or he is referring to criminal and civil disputes. The phrase in 8 may make the same distinction as in 1 ('either a whole tribe or an individual'), or both terms refer to individuals acting either in a public or in a private capacity.

2 **religiōnēs:** this is a difficult word to translate, because it denotes not only the doctrines of a religion, but all the phenomena associated with it, such as signs and omens, and (as in the final extract) the feelings of the worshippers.

11 **impiōrum ac scelestōrum:** the law-breakers formed the lowest social class among the Celts, who did not practise slavery; they were not imprisoned but lost their civil rights.

19 **disciplīna:** another difficult word; here and in 32 it implies a body of knowledge, a system of belief and a way of life. In 26 it signifies instruction in the wisdom and knowledge of the Druids, or even, possibly, the place where such instruction was given.
in Britanniā reperta: the fact that no trace of Druidism has been found in Cisalpine Gaul lends support to this belief. Druidism was possibly a pre-Celtic institution first systematically organised in Britain and then adopted by the conquering Celts. Some authorities regard Caesar as wrong on this point, arguing that the Druids were the unifying force throughout the Celtic world.

21 **eam rem:** i.e. the *disciplīnam*.

Their education

23 **tribūta:** taxes were paid by all tribesmen who worked their own land. These taxes, as today, were used to fund all the public works and institutions (it is becoming clear from archaeology that Celtic civilisation was surprisingly advanced).

24-5 **omnium...rērum immūnitātem:** 'exemption from all duties'.

30 **Graecīs litterīs:** it is thought that they learned the Greek alphabet through contact with the Greek colony at Massilia (modern Marseille).

34-5 **animās...trānsīre:** another borrowing from, or lending to, the Greek world, where Pythagorean philosophy had similar beliefs. In fact, Aristotle states that the early Greek philosophers borrowed much of their philosophy from the Celts.

35 **hōc:** ablative of instrument, referring to the belief in the immortality of the soul.

Their religion

40 **dēdita religiōnibus:** there is evidence that the Celts were thoroughgoing animists: bogs, springs, rivers, groves and many other natural features were regarded as the sacred homes of deities. An immense number of local and tribal gods appears to have existed throughout

110   *Commentary: prose selections*

the Celtic world, often reflected in Roman coupling of native and Roman deities.

43 hominēs immolant: many ancient authors mention the Druidic practice of human sacrifice and it is widely believed that this was the principal reason why the Druids were targeted for extermination by the Romans. In addition to the wickerwork cages, Strabo mentions ritual sacrifice by archery and crucifixion. There is, however, no direct archaeological evidence to corroborate this practice: decapitated bodies discovered at several sites are more probably to be explained as being trophies resulting from warfare. An alternative reason for the persecution of the Druids by the Romans is their effective opposition to Roman rule. Allegations of human sacrifice, whether well-founded or not, offered the Romans a convenient pretext for persecution.

47 aliī: Caesar gives no indication of the identity of these 'others'.

The Druids' last stand (Extracts from Tacitus, *Annals* XIV.29-30)

Tacitus provides little background to the attack on Anglesey. The episode appears to function as hardly more than a backdrop for the revolt of Boudica. We are told that Suetonius, being newly appointed to the post of governor in AD 59, wished to gain an immediate victory to match those that Corbulo was currently winning against the Parthians in his reconquest of Armenia.

2 receptāculum perfugārum: just as, in the time of Julius Caesar, the outlawed Druids had fled from Gaul westwards to Britain, so, in the face of the Roman conquest of Britain, they were forced to seek refuge in remote areas still beyond the reach of the legionaries. Evidence of the importance of Anglesey to the Druids comes from a contemporary hoard of iron, bronze and wooden objects found in peat below a lake at Llyn Cerrig Bach in 1943.

3 stābat: note the emphatic position of the word; the Latin word order may be retained in translation: 'standing on the...was...'.

5 intercursantibus fēminīs: Celtic women had much more freedom than Roman women, enjoying full equality of rights. For their presence at battles, see **Boudica's rebellion** in **tumultus et rebelliō**, p.172.

11-12 **ignī suō:** *suō* here refers not, of course, to the grammatical subject (the Romans) but the subject uppermost in the writer's mind (the Britons).

13 **lūcī...sacrī:** sacred groves were a regular feature of Celtic religion (see note on 40 above and 3 of **Mistletoe**). These groves appeared to the Romans to be a significant focus of Druidic, anti-Roman influence.

saevīs superstitiōnibus sacrī: 'devoted to barbaric rites', i.e. to human sacrifices.

14-15 **hominum fibrīs cōnsulere deōs:** this practice, of divining the will of the gods by the examination of a victim's entrails, was similar to the Roman practice of *dīvīnātiō*, in which the *haruspex* interpreted the liver of a sacrificed animal. Here Tacitus clearly intends to shock the reader with the idea of a human victim.

Mistletoe (Extracts from Pliny, Natural History XVI.249-51)

The *Natural History,* in 37 volumes, is one of the most important prose works written in Latin because of the wealth of information it contains about so many aspects of Roman culture. Although not the result of primary research or observation, it is a skilful synthesis of facts and opinions from one hundred major and four hundred minor authors. Books XII-XIX are devoted to botany, including trees and agriculture.

1 **magōs:** it is interesting that Pliny chooses this word rather than *sacerdōtēs; magus* was usually applied by Roman authors to the learned men and priests of the Persians. Here perhaps Pliny wants a different name for men whose practices he regarded as quaint and un-Roman.

2 **viscō:** mistletoe was regarded as a mysterious magical plant. It was thought that it could cure disease, protect from evil and stimulate fertility (as here). In Virgil's *Aeneid* and in Norse legend it opens the gates of Hell. It was thought to live through killing its source of life and thus to encompass life and death at the same time. Until the

middle of the 19th century it was believed to be effective against epilepsy.

3 **per sē:** i.e. the Druids chose the groves even if there was no mistletoe growing on the trees. The purpose for which they chose them is unclear, but may refer to sacred rites.

6 **rārō...invenītur:** mistletoe grows most frequently on the apple tree.

7-8 **quae prīncipia...facit:** this seems to mean that the Celts reckoned their months and years from the sixth day of a new moon. The Druids' advanced knowledge of physics and astronomy enabled them to construct more sophisticated calendars than the Julian one currently in use in Rome. For a detailed account of Celtic science, including the famous Coligny Calendar, see Peter Beresford Ellis, *Caesar's Invasion of Britain* (Orbic), pp.30ff.

10 **candidōs taurōs:** c.f. the *candentem taurum* promised to the gods by Cloanthus in return for victory in the boat race in *Aeneid* V, 236. The emphasis on whiteness here, together with the white berry of the mistletoe, perhaps symbolises the white light of the moon. The binding of the horns, presumably with wreaths, was a prelude to sacrifice.

12 **falce aureā:** gold would have been too soft to cut the tough stems; the sickles more probably would have been made of gilded bronze.

14 **prosperum faciat:** i.e. the deity should bestow success on those who offered up the sacrifice.

15 **eīs quibus dederit:** i.e. those to whom the deity has given the gift of mistletoe.

17 **rēbus frīvolīs:** Pliny shows bias here.

Discussion

A suitable approach to this topic is to compare the treatment of the three writers. The first two sections of Caesar's account describe a well-ordered and sophisticated society in which the Druids fill the rôles of teacher, judge and priest. The third section, however, gives a contrasting picture of barbaric rites which suggests a degree of inconsistency in Caesar's sources or in his interpretation of them. There has been some speculation whether the view, common among Roman writers, that the Celts possessed sophisticated cultural, religious and philosophical systems is the result of the natural tendency of classical writers to imbue other societies with their own *mores*. (Caesar's main source was the Stoic philosopher Posidonius, who may have projected his own philosophical beliefs on the Celtic society he described.) There can be no doubt, however, of the Druids' knowledge of calendars; they may even have inherited the calendrical and astronomical knowledge now increasingly associated with Stonehenge. Similarities between the Druidic and Pythagorean doctrines of metempsychosis may have been exaggerated but the literary record is so consistent that there must have been some resemblance. That the Druids practised human sacrifice was widely believed in the Roman world, and was the principal reason for their being outlawed. Archaeological evidence, however, points only to the widespread cult of the severed head, which does not necessarily imply sacrifice. We are left, therefore, with the question of how much of Caesar's account is the result of personal observation, and how much is unacknowledged borrowing from other sources.

Tacitus' account of the battle on the shores of Anglesey is briefly stated, forming no more than an introduction to the career in Britain of Suetonius and to the historically more significant revolt of Boudica (pp.170-4); the factual note on the Britons' religious practices forms the briefest appendix to this introduction. His language, in contrast to Caesar's, is emotive and full of imagery: the overall picture - or sequence of pictures - is more important than its component facts. Pupils may wish to isolate individual scenes from within the sequence and assess their effect in isolation and in combination. The description appears to 'zoom in' upon the Druids' army as the Romans approach across the strait. Was Tacitus trying to entertain, to shock, or merely to give the facts? Determining the historical accuracy of his facts is often next to impossible, even when he lists his sources. Expert opinion, however, holds that Tacitus has rarely been disproved in the matter of facts, as opposed to interpretation. He could have had access to the memoirs of Suetonius and to the first-hand accounts of his father-in-law, Agricola, who served under Suetonius during these events; but the reference to human sacrifice could equally be unverified rumour.

Pliny's account of mistletoe, certainly taken from earlier but unidentified sources (though, like Caesar, he used Posidonius), is concerned more with the plant than the people who used it; indeed, he is dismissive of the uses to which it is put (*rēbus frīvolīs*). Pliny was not in the habit of calling his sources into question, accepting any material which was not anomalous. We can do no more than assess the extent to which this account conforms to the picture of the Druids we have constructed from other sources. It is certain that natural features such as trees and plants were sacred to the Celts; whether the oak was actually among these, or merely assumed to be so by classical authors linking the etymology of the word *Druides* to the Greek *drus* (oak tree) is less certain. It will be noted that certain of the rituals described here are paralleled in the Graeco-Roman world (see, for example, L.Whibley, *A Companion to Greek Studies*, CUP, pp.405f.); this again raises the question of cultural objectivity in Pliny's original source: are the beliefs underpinning the rituals genuinely Celtic or no more than Graeco-Roman extrapolation? Such questions remain unanswerable because of the lack of corroborative evidence; Celtic literature is unfortunately lacking.

Pupil discussion could begin with a comparison of the credibility of the three sources: which bits are most or least believable? Does any of the three authors seem particularly (un)trustworthy? A more specific question could explore the extent to which Tacitus' corroboration of Caesar's account of the Druids' practice of human sacrifice adds to their authenticity - or are there reasons for distrusting them both? Pupils might then consider what Caesar, Pliny and their readers found interesting about the Druids: do they feel the same interest? Why do modern Druids arouse so much interest in the media and among the general public?

tumultus et rebelliō

The riot at Pompeii (Extracts from Tacitus, *Annals* XIV.17)

1 **sub idem tempus:** Tacitus has just been describing Nero's public demonstrations of his supposed artistic talents, in AD 59.

ātrōx...levī: the antithesis emphasises how quickly and easily such incidents can escalate in violence.

2 **Nūcerīnōs:** Nuceria (modern Nocera) lay on the *via Appia* 9 miles east of Pompeii, which acted as its harbour.

gladiātōriō spectāculō: 'at a gladiatorial show', an ablative of time or place.

3 **Līvinēius Rēgulus:** the circumstances surrounding his expulsion from the senate are now lost.

oppidānī...solitā lascīviā: Tacitus is suggesting that such vociferous exchanges of obscenities were more typical of townsfolk than of the urban proletariat, perhaps because the means of enforcing crowd control were more immediately available in Rome because of the presence there of the praetorian guard and the *vigilēs* (combined firemen and policemen). Or is Tacitus being snobbish?

4–5 **probra...sūmpsērunt:** note the stages in the escalation, from provocative verbal abuse (*probra*) to stones and then to swords. A similar escalation may be observed today in football matches, where deaths are not unknown. Probably in both situations the games are secondary to the gratuitous violence. The use of a single verb governing three objects is an example of syllepsis.

5 **validiōre Pompēiānōrum plēbe:** presumably because the show was being given in Pompeii, the locals were in the majority. Also, it was a 'home match' for the Pompeians, but an 'away fixture' for the Nucerians!

apud quōs: 'in whose town'.

7 **dēportātī sunt:** the injured Nucerians were taken to Rome to give evidence to the inquiry of the seriousness of the incident.

8 **līberōrum aut parentum:** this reminds us that such shows, like football matches, were occasions for family outings.

8-10 iūdicium...relātā: the riot must have been viewed seriously for it to have been referred directly to Nero; the delegation of the inquiry to the senate and then to the consuls was quite normal, since the senate sat as a court of law and cases were prepared and presented by the consuls.

10 eius modī coetū: i.e. gladiatorial shows. The length of the ban suggests that the senate, and beyond it the emperor, regarded the riot as more than an isolated incident. Tacitus also implies that there were illicit *collēgia* at Pompeii and that they were involved in violence. Roman emperors had a perennial aversion to *collēgia*, which were rigorously circumscribed, and at times proscribed, by legislation. Under Nero, *collēgia* were only permitted, by individual sanction of the senate or the emperor, if they served a definite public utility and were non-political. (In a well-known pair of letters, X.33 and X.34, Pliny is forbidden by Trajan from maintaining a fire-brigade in Nicomedia because the emperor feared that it would become a political club.) The severity of the penalty reflects the determination of the central government to impose and maintain law and order in country towns.

12-13 sēditiōnem concīverant: these are strong words, suggesting that Regulus and others had established illicit *collēgia* and deliberately provoked the violence as part of a new political campaign after his expulsion from the senate. Exile was therefore an appropriate punishment.

Discussion

There can be no doubt that the riot was viewed seriously by the authorities in Rome; whether the people of Pompeii were offended more by the penalties than by the riot is more difficult to say: the only evidence is the wall-painting of the riot (see *Cambridge Latin Course* Stage 8) and several graffiti which may or may not be contemporary. Tacitus leaves us to draw our own conclusions about the intentions of Regulus, but the implications are clear enough. Tacitus also reflects the policy of the centralised authority, whose interest outweighs that of the provincial town. Something of his own political and social persuasion emerges from his choice of words and imagery, which emphasise the horrific consequences of the riot and the threat to public order posed by unscrupulous and influential men like Regulus.

Pupils might consider the harshness or otherwise of the sentence, especially insofar as it applies to Regulus. They might also think of examples of similar riots today and discuss the differences in penalties imposed now. Why are football clubs not banned for ten years?

Boudica's rebellion (Extracts from Tacitus, *Annals* XIV.31-7)

1 **Icenōrum:** the Iceni occupied Norfolk and parts of neighbouring counties with their capital possibly near Norwich.

   Prasutagus: he had recently died and, having no son, had vainly attempted to safeguard his family and kingdom by making Nero co-heir. Prasutagus had been given the status of client king by Claudius, but this status had probably lapsed on Claudius' death in AD 54. Prasutagus' death would have left Boudica with no official status in the eyes of the Romans, since imperial policy stated that the property of a client king passed to Rome on his death, unless the Romans chose to confer client-king status on his heir.

3 **quod:** connecting relative.

5 **servīs:** whereas the centurions represented the military authority vested in the governor, the slaves were on the staff of the procurator, who supervised taxation.

   velut capta: i.e. like a prize of war.

7 **mūnerī:** 'as a gift' (predicative dative).

10 **in fōrmam prōvinciae:** i.e. they had lost their client-kingdom status and attendant privileges; as part of the province they would have to tolerate the imposition of Roman customs, institutions and tribute. It was just this heavy-handed treatment that had so incensed the Trinobantes.

13-14 **veterānōs...colōniam:** Camulodunum (Colchester) was the tribal capital of the Trinobantes. The first *colōnia* had been established there in AD 49 for veterans of the Twentieth Legion. The recent contingent had probably been retired from the same legion before its departure to Anglesey to quell the Druids in 59. Every new group of veterans needed land, and the Romans had no scruples about dispossessing the native landowning aristocracy.

16 **mīlitēs:** although the veterans themselves were meant to provide a military presence in the town, there were in addition a few legionary soldiers on guard duty. In theory, these should have restrained the activities of the veterans, but they naturally supported their fellows against the barbarians.

17 **similitūdine, spē:** probably causal ablatives. The soldiers sympathised with the veterans being of the same profession.

18 **templum...exstrūctum:** it is possible that Claudius commissioned the temple immediately after the capture of Camulodunum in 43, but more likely that it was begun only after his death and subsequent deification in 54.

19 **ēlēctīque sacerdōtēs:** worship of the emperor would have taken place at a series of festivals throughout the year. These festivals were expensive to stage and the cost usually was borne by the priests. As the Romans had no intention of incurring unnecessary expenses in a barbarian land, they recruited the priests from among the local nobility, forcing them to pay for the supposed privilege of worshipping the symbol of their own oppression.

21-2 **nūllīs mūnīmentīs saeptam:** this seems surprising for the Roman provincial capital, but archaeology has revealed that the fortifications of the original fortress, within which the *colōnia* was established, were levelled: the Romans must have been very confident of their supremacy.

22 **ducibus nostrīs:** dative of the agent.

25-6 **decem...mīlia armātōrum:** i.e. 10,000 troops in all: a small enough force in the face of up to 100,000 rebel warriors. The only other force available to Suetonius was the Second Legion, probably stationed in their new fortress at Exeter; the acting commander of this legion, fearing the strength of the enemy, refused Suetonius' appeals to join him.

27 **locum...clausum:** the place he chose was the upper end of a broad valley or plain, so that his rear and flanks were defended from enemy attack by the narrow wooded defile; furthermore, the Britons would be forced to advance into a place of diminishing width, where their superior numbers would be of no advantage to them. The exact site is uncertain, but may have been at Mancetter near Atherstone on Watling Street, along which both armies would have had to march to meet each other.

30 **frequentēs ōrdinibus:** 'in close formation'.

32-3 **passim...exultābant:** Tacitus paints a picture of wild disorder among the British forces, which their commanders would have found impossible to control.

34 **testēs:** 'as witnesses'.

37 **gradū immōta:** 'not moving from its position'.

38 **certō iactū:** i.e. with deadly effect.

40-1 **perfringunt...erat:** indefinite: 'they broke through any strong forces in their path'.

46-8 **sunt quī...vulnerātīs:** *trādant* is generic subjunctive. It is interesting that Tacitus did not take the trouble to consult the most reliable source, the memoirs of Suetonius Paulinus himself. Such exaggeration, together with his brief and selective description of the battle, suits his dramatic style and depicts in the most vivid colours the picture of the clash between Roman and barbarian.

49 **venēnō:** according to Dio, she fell ill and died; the two versions, however, are not necessarily incompatible.

Discussion

Tacitus' description of the revolt forms only a small interlude in a long account of the reign of Nero: there is no reason to suppose that at least in the context of a History of Rome he thought there was anything particularly remarkable in the episode, which he treats like many others, in a sketchy manner, content to draw out the main themes. This explains why there are so many questions left unanswered. Such uncertainties include the details of Suetonius' march from Wales, the site of the battle, the personalities of the two leaders and some details of imperial policy towards Britain. One view of Tacitus is that he saw the writing of history as a means of presenting in dramatic form what he considered to be important moral themes of the day, and so episodes such as Boudica's revolt are written in such a way as to maximise their dramatic effect. Another view might be that the dramatic nature of his narrative is his way of presenting historical facts in a readable manner; a remote province such as Britain simply did not merit a more detailed account.

The events of the revolt are presented in a factual way with little comment from the historian. One may speculate whether he viewed with distaste the violent treatment of Boudica and her daughters by the Roman soldiers and public slaves: his use of emotive words such as *vāstārentur* and *contumēliā*, and his detailed catalogue of grievances, support this view. Another fruitful question for class discussion is the place of justice: were the Iceni and the Trinobantes justified in rebelling against the oppression of Roman rule, or were the Romans justified in regarding the Britons as little more than savages with no special rights under the law?

Pupils might be asked whether Tacitus' account of the final battle suggests any reason why the Romans, though outnumbered, won; they might note, for example, that the Britons' over-confidence in 33 contributes to their disastrous defeat in 41.

Unrest at Ephesus (*Acts of the Apostles* XIX.24–41)

This passage is taken from the Latin translation of the Bible known as the Vulgate. It was made by Jerome at the end of the fourth century AD to meet the need for a Latin version as Christianity spread westwards across the Mediterranean.

- 1-2 **aedēs argenteās:** these were miniature replicas bought as souvenirs.
- 2 **nōn modicum:** the litotes helps to emphasise the economic importance of Demetrius and, through him, of the cult of Diana.
- 5-6 **tōtius Asiae:** locative by attraction to *Ephesī*.
- 6 **āvertisse:** *lit.* 'has enticed a large crowd away' (from the worship of Diana).
- 7 **nōn sunt deī quī manibus fiunt:** a central tenet of Christianity.

8-11 perīculum erit...colit: note the mixture of economic self-interest and religious obligation in Demetrius' arguments.

9 Diānae templum: the temple of Diana at Ephesus was built after 356 BC on the site of earlier temples; it was the centre of the Asiatic cult of a fertility goddess early identified by the Greeks with Artemis and one of the Seven Wonders of the Ancient World.

14 in theātrum: the theatre, still very well-preserved, stood on a hillside close by the street of the silversmiths' shops. It was of considerable size, accommodating 25,000 people, and was regularly used for the constitutional assembly of citizens.

16 intrāre in populum: i.e. to enter the theatre and talk to the people assembled there.

discipulī: when Paul first arrived at Ephesus, he found twelve men who had already become Christians; these men are referred to as *discipulī*.

17 Asiae prīncipibus: also known by their Greek name as Asiarchs, they were Roman officials whose task was to encourage emperor worship. Their own lack of success in overcoming the resistance of the Jews and worshippers of Diana in Asia caused them to appreciate the achievement of Paul in winning so many converts to Christianity.

20-5 Religious tensions are evident here: the Hellenised cult of Diana, the Jews and the Christian Paul are all competing for followers. Alexander was probably of Greek origin, and so would be expected to be a devotee of Diana, whose worshippers, forming the majority of those present, would be shocked to discover his Jewish persuasion.

30 hominēs istōs: i.e. Gaius and Aristarchus.

32-3 conventūs forēnsēs aguntur: 'law courts are held'; the *conventūs* were, strictly speaking, judicial circuits into which the provinces were divided; there were at least twelve in the province of Asia, one of which would certainly have been at Ephesus, the provincial capital.

prōcōnsulēs sunt: 'there are proconsuls'; the proconsul was the Roman governor of the province. One of his duties was to visit the *conventūs* in sequence, like a modern circuit judge.

34 lēgitimā ecclēsiā: i.e. as opposed to the unconstitutional assembly in the theatre.

36 dē quō: 'on whose account'; a guilty person would provide some justification for a disorderly assembly.

Discussion

This piece may be explored as an example of religious tension in a multi-ethnic community. Ephesus, with a population of about 250,000, was a prosperous city comprising several distinct cultures. Jews and followers of Diana had co-existed peacefully until the arrival of a third, actively proselytising cult inimical to both. In the background stood the official cult of the emperor of Rome. The interrelationship between religion and local economy is also interesting: one might compare the similar economic reliance on religious fervour in such modern Christian centres as Lourdes (would Paul have approved of this?). Pupils might like to speculate on the nationality of the *scrība*: he does not take sides, rather looking to the established, i.e. Roman, authorities to provide a solution. His use of *vestram* in 31 implies that he is not Greek, but unfortunately this reading is contested.

The passage raises many questions which are difficult, if not impossible, to answer. We are not told why Alexander was picked on (21) or why the Greeks were disconcerted to find that he was a Jew. The sudden appearance of the *scrība* is unexplained, as is his reference to *aliae rēs* (34).

Pupils could be asked to trace the growth of the disturbance from the protests of Demetrius to the general disturbance culminating in the march to the theatre. What started as a trade dispute ended as a situation threatening the rule of law in the city. It is interesting that many of the crowd did not know why they were there; is this typical of crowd-formation? Pupils might also wish to know what happened to Paul afterwards.

APPENDIX A: NOTES ON THE ILLUSTRATIONS

1 *Orpheus and Eurydice* by the Victorian artist G.F.Watts
George Frederick Watts (1817-1904), remarkably for the son of an unsuccessful Marylebone piano-maker and tuner, found early patronage and fame as a painter. Like many Victorians, he was fascinated by Greek and Roman themes; they gave him scope for pictures with symbolic and moral meanings (he was himself an austere and high-minded person). In this painting of 1879, Watts tackles the destructiveness of possessive love. The daylight, striking the cave wall and the figures from the left, shows that Orpheus is nearly back to the surface and safety. Watts tries to suggest the moment when Eurydice, almost a solid living woman once more, begins to fade again into a spirit, as the pale flesh fades into shadow and the drapery, especially below the knee, merges with the rock. The drapery may owe something to the Parthenon pediment figures in the British Museum, which Watts much admired. (Aberdeen Art Gallery)

6 The lovers' last farewell, as Mercury (at left) stands ready to draw Eurydice back to the Underworld
This relief (cast in the Museum of Classical Archaeology, Cambridge, from the original in the Naples Museum) is a Roman copy of a Classical Greek original. Orpheus on the right carries his lyre; his face has been restored. Mercury (Hermes) the Escorter of Souls (*Psychopompos*) is recognisable by his traveller's hat; he takes Eurydice by her right hand; her left rests on Orpheus' shoulder, as he lightly touches her wrist and the two gaze at each other in an instant of stillness before they are swept apart. The original has been attributed to Callimachos, a contemporary and follower of Pheidias (the designer of the Parthenon sculptures). Like Pheidias he carved drapery with subtlety. Contrast the quiet, untheatrical composition with Watts' (p.1); which is more moving?

10 A female follower of Bacchus beats her tambour
This Bacchante is a detail from a mosaic of the Triumph of Bacchus at Sousse, Tunisia. The god's followers are frequently shown beating

drums to help create the ecstatic frenzy in which they tore animals - and Orpheus - to pieces.

19 Battle scene from an Etruscan pottery urn, made for the ashes of a dead warrior
Thanks to archaeology, we can see in museums actual objects and paintings from the age of the Trojan War. Roman authors would not have known these and would have formed their mental image of the ancient heroes from Greek or earlier Italian art (and of course from Homer and other literature). This and the next illustration are taken from objects from the Italian civilisations, from which elements of Roman culture were derived; this Etruscan ashchest, from Chiusi, is in the British Museum. It was made in the 2nd century BC and is brightly painted in red, blue, yellow and other colours; a young man, reclining for a banquet, is modelled on the lid (not shown), with below it the name: Thana Ancarui Thelesa. The tightly-knit group of five warriors, lightly clad and armed with helmets, swords and circular shields, is influenced by Hellenistic Greek sculpture (the school of Pergamum).

24 Warriors carrying a dead comrade
This is the cast bronze handle of the lid from a cylindrical box (*cista*) from Praeneste (the modern Palestrina), a great centre of bronze working. Two bearded warriors with helmets, breastplates, greaves and lances, carry the body of a young comrade. Late 4th century BC. (Rome, Villa Giulia Museum)

25 Cupid, behind Narcissus' shoulder, tempts him to love only his own reflections
The story of Echo and Narcissus was evidently popular at Pompeii and the Naples Museum has several wall paintings of it, including this one.

33 Narcissus flowers spring up beside the head of the dying hero in this 17th-century French painting by Nicolas Poussin
Poussin has tried to suggest Echo turning into stone (line 36) by painting her faintly in the same brown as the rock behind her. As in the

Roman painting, Cupid is present to symbolise love (bearing a torch). 'With its smouldering evening sky and gradually waning light, the picture breathes the very atmosphere of romantic loss' (Richard Verdi, *Nicolas Poussin 1594-1665,* Royal Academy 1995). The painting is in the Louvre.

34 A Victorian view of Echo and Narcissus

The Pre-Raphaelite painter John William Waterhouse (1849-1917) specialised in mythic paintings with a romantic, dreamy mood; his Echo has a characteristically wistful look as Narcissus immerses himself in his own reflection. Contrast with the Poussin. (Walker Art Gallery, Liverpool)

38 *Jupiter and Mercury visiting Philemon and Baucis* by Rembrandt van Rijn

Rembrandt van Rijn (1606-69) painted this in 1658. He uses a dramatic contrast of shadow penetrated by weak light from a single source, appropriately in the aged couple's humble cottage; the light forms a halo behind Mercury's head and spills most richly onto Jupiter, establishing the authority of the two visitors without breaching their disguise. The youthful Mercury leans forward with concern as Baucis proffers the goose; at left, the fire she has coaxed into being (lines 15ff.) glows dimly. The closeness of the couple to each other is evident, as well as their humility. (Washington DC, National Gallery of Art)

42 Goose

This goose is taken from a North African mosaic villa scene, shown in full on p.61.

46 Terracotta of lovers

A terracotta statuette of a couple embracing, from Pompeii and in the Naples Museum. Such statuettes may have been made as New Year's gifts, for the Saturnalia.

52 Detail of Arretine vase, lovers

Detail of a cast of an Arretine vase of the late 1st century BC, made by Marcus Perennius. Perennius was the leading manufacturer of the glossy red ware whose manufacture spread widely from Arretium (Arezzo), and is commonly known as 'samian'. This vase belongs to the period of Horace and Ovid and was made for use at rich men's parties; Perennius was expert at showing lovemaking without degenerating into pornography (see Catherine Johns, *Sex or Symbol?*, British Museum Press 1982, pp.124ff.).

56 lectō compositus...
57 ...cum mē saevus Amor...

These two images are in reality totally disconnected. The first comes from the lid of a tomb in the Museo Nazionale Romano (the Terme Museum), so that the young man is on his deathbed; he holds an egg in his hand (not shown) as a promise of future life. The Cupid with the appraising look in the eye is a detail from a sarcophagus with the story of Phaedra; the god is really watching the nurse whispering to the lovesick queen.

60 As it is: the remains of Horace's villa at Licenza

Horace gives quite precise details of the location and characteristics of his cherished villa in the Sabine Hills, and this villa fits them well. The villa was presented to him by Maecenas. We are looking roughly NE across the main block of the building, the apsidal room in the foreground being part of the bath suite. Dining rooms and bedrooms were at the far end, beyond two courtyards with fountains. To the right was a large enclosed garden.

61 As it was: a Roman country house in North Africa

This mosaic is from a Roman villa in Tabarka, Tunisia, and is now in the Bardo Museum, Tunis. The house stands in a park full of birds, trees and flowers.

64 Perfume container
This tiny bronze vessel, under 10 cm high, could have been used to contain perfume. It is Greek work of the 2nd or 1st century BC and the sensitive modelling of the head of an African girl would no doubt have appealed to Catullus. (British Museum)

66 Bone rings decorated with theatre masks
These rings are in the Ashmolean Museum, Oxford.

70 Tipsy worshippers
This is a detail from a painting taken from a columbarium (burial chamber) in the Villa Pamphili, Rome, and now in the British Museum. Though it actually portrays worshippers of Bacchus, no doubt the devotees of Anna Perenna would be in much the same state after taking a cup of wine for each year they hoped to live (lines 9-10).

74 The four seasons appear at the corners of this mosaic floor
This is another mosaic from Africa, in the Bardo Museum. The central scene shows Apollo and Marsyas competing, but the picture has been included for the roundels at the corners portraying the four seasons, a very frequent theme in art as in poetry (lines 11-12). The seasons run clockwise from Spring at top left. See also pp.90 and 92.

78 The spring of Bandusia
If Horace's villa has been correctly identified, this spring nearby is probably the *fōns Bandusiae*.

80 Mouse and walnut
A detail from a mosaic of an unswept floor (*asaroton*) apparently littered with the remains of last night's banquet, among which this mouse forages. The design was originated by the Hellenistic artist Sosos of Pergamum. (Vatican Museum)

84 Hunting dog
This detail from a mosaic of a hare hunt makes clear what might have scared off the Country Mouse; found in Roman Carthage. (Bardo Museum, Tunis)

88 An outdoor dining room, Pompeii
Martial's simple but civilised lifestyle is evoked by this 19th-century woodcut of the summer triclinium of the House of Sallust in Pompeii; the table is of marble and the three couches are shaded by a trellis.

90 Summer
Detail from a mosaic of the four seasons (see p.74): summer, wreathed with ears of corn. Carthage, 4th century AD. (Bardo Museum, Tunis)

92 Winter
Detail from a mosaic of the four seasons: Winter, with a bare branch. (Bignor Roman Villa, Sussex)

102 Germanicus, on a coin of his son, the Emperor Caligula
This bronze dupondius commemorates Germanicus' triumph, celebrated after he recovered the legionary standards lost to the Germans in battle by Varus in the reign of Augustus. (British Museum)

103 The head of Germanicus on a coin of Caligula
The coin is a bronze *as*. (British Museum)

104 Agrippina, wife of Germanicus
Bronze sestertius of Caligula. (British Museum)

106 The death of Germanicus (detail), Nicolas Poussin
This very influential painting of 1626-8, now in the Minneapolis Institute of Arts, introduced a new theme to art - the hero on his deathbed. We see the moment before Germanicus' soldiers, at left, touch his right hand, which lies on his chest, and swear the oath Tacitus describes (lines 26ff.). Agrippina sits at right, head bowed and her face

concealed; the artist had probably read Pliny the Elder, who notes that this pose had been used by the Greek painter Timanthes because the profoundest sorrow could only be suggested, not depicted (see Verdi, R., *op. cit.*, p.163).

113 Messalina
This coin of the reign of Claudius, a silver didrachm, was minted in Caesarea.

120 Claudius
A sardonyx cameo in the British Museum, showing the emperor wearing a cuirass and military cloak. The features seem sensitively carved but ineffectual.

121 Messalina and her children
Another cameo, in the Bibliothèque Nationale, Paris. Her children are shown too, their heads emerging from horns of plenty: Britannicus (right) who is apparently intended to resemble Augustus, and Octavia who is portrayed, like Livia frequently, helmeted as the goddess Roma.

124 Initial letters from a 15th-century manuscript of Pliny the Elder's *Natural History*
This fascinating manuscript is in the Victoria and Albert Museum, London. The illuminated initials have been attributed to Giuliano Amedei. The picture of Pliny the Elder - dressed in 15th-century clothing and not in any sense a true portrait - decorates Book I, in which Pliny lists the contents and sources of each book of his encyclopedic work; he claims to have recorded some 20,000 noteworthy facts. Opposite is a selection of details from some of the other 36 books. The picture for Book IX *On Aquatic Species* includes Nereids or mermaids (Pliny claimed to know of proof of their existence) - there are two mermaids in the picture as well as a sea-centaur, dolphin, octopus and various other creatures. For Book XXXIV *On Copper, Bronze, Lead,*

etc., the illuminator has drawn four men hammering a metal dish, while a furnace burns in the background at right. Book VII *On the Human Race* includes a man with his eye in the middle of his body, far right, and an Umbrella-Foot in the foreground - a member of a fabulous tribe that use their big feet to shade them from the sun, and Book XXVI *On various Drugs* shows a doctor and his assistant attending a sick man. Illustrated in colour in J.I.Whalley, *Pliny the Elder: Historia Naturalis* (Victoria and Albert Museum 1982).

128 An 18th-century eruption of Vesuvius
Vesuvius erupting, painted by Joseph Wright of Derby after returning from Italy in 1775. (Derby Museums and Art Gallery)

133 A visit to a sorceress
This is a detail from a very finely-worked mosaic panel found in the 'Villa of Cicero' at Pompeii and now in the Naples Museum; it was probably made in the 2nd century BC. Dioscurides of Samos, who signed it, was probably copying a 3rd-century Greek painting. It is a scene from a comedy. The two women to the left have probably come to consult a 'wise woman' about an affair of the heart; the old witch holds a goblet - of wine perhaps, or it may be a love potion. The enquirers' hands register the tension of the encounter. A servant girl stands at right.

140 A witch giving a potion to a client
The interpretation of this wall-painting from the House of the Dioscuri in Pompeii is disputed. The description adopted here follows the suggestion of Maiuri.

143 A mourning woman
This funerary statue was found in the necropolis outside the Nuceria Gate at Pompeii. It represents a type of womanhood, dignified and rather severe, to which Arria would no doubt consider herself belonging. 1st century AD.

Appendix A   131

150 Ivory relief of a pantomime performer
This relief in Berlin (4th century AD) shows a female pantomimist, who would dance and mime all the roles while a chorus sang the story. She carries the masks of a hero, a heroine and a youth, and as props she has a sword, crown and lyre.

153 A basket of fish
This mosaic of a basket with an abundant catch of fish was made in Roman Carthage in the 1st or 2nd century AD. It may be from the floor of a dining room. (British Museum)

159 Villa by the seaside
This is a painting from Stabiae which shows a typical seaside villa - a two-storey building jutting out into the sea, with a rectangular garden surrounded by a portico on three sides, and trees rising behind the house. 1st century AD.

161 Skull
See following note.

164 Gateway of a Celtic sanctuary in Gaul
This is the top of a gateway from Roquepertuse (Bouches-du-Rhône), which led into a sanctuary. In the uprights there are several oval recesses (two shown in our picture) which contain skulls, possibly those of prisoners killed in battle, rather than sacrificed in the way that Caesar describes. 2nd century BC. (Historical Museum, Marseille)

168 Graffito from Pompeii about the riot in the amphitheatre
The inscription reads: CAMPANI VICTORIA VNA/NVCERINIS PERISTIS, 'O Campanians, you have perished in the hour of victory, together with the Nucerians [or, in one victory].' Above it on the right, clearly drawn, is a victorious gladiator holding the palm-branch symbol of victory. On the left, clumsily indicated by another hand, a figure appears to drag another up a ladder or flight of steps.

174 The statue of Boudica by the Thames in London
The famous statue of Boudica (Boadicea) in her scythe-wheeled chariot was made by Thomas Thorneycroft. With her daughters she rides to revenge, horses rearing.

177 The Great Theatre at Ephesus
This theatre, in which the Ephesians held their tumultuous assembly, was a vast building, holding some 56,000 people. As remodelled in Roman times, it had a raised stage and an elaborate architectural background (*scaenae frōns*) with several tiers of columns and statues.

APPENDIX B: METRICAL SCHEMES

The basic metrical schemes of the verse passages in the pupil's text are as follows:

1 Hexameter

$$\left.\frac{-\cup\cup}{--}\right|\left.\frac{-\cup\cup}{--}\right|\left.\frac{-\cup\cup}{--}\right|\left.\frac{-\cup\cup}{--}\right|-\cup\cup\,\underline{\cup}$$

2 Elegiac couplet
   1st line hexameter
   2nd line pentameter

$$\left.\frac{-\cup\cup}{--}\right|\left.\frac{-\cup\cup}{--}\right|-\left\|-\cup\cup\right|-\cup\cup\left|\underline{\cup}\right.$$

3 Third asclepiad

$$--\left|-\cup\cup-\right|-\cup\cup-\left|\cup\underline{\cup}\right.$$
$$--\left|-\cup\cup-\right|-\cup\cup-\left|\cup\underline{\cup}\right.$$
$$--\left|-\cup\cup-\right|-$$
$$--\left|-\cup\cup-\right|\cup\underline{\cup}$$

4 Hendecasyllables

$$--\left|-\cup\cup-\left|\cup-\cup\,\underline{\cup}\right.\right.$$
$$-\cup$$
$$\cup-$$

5 Iambic trimeter and dimeter

$$\cup-\cup-\left|\overset{\cup\cup\cup}{\underset{-}{\cup}}-\cup-\left|\cup-\cup\underline{\cup}\right.\right.$$

$$\cup-\cup-\left|\underset{-}{\cup}-\cup\underline{\cup}\right.$$

6 Sapphic

$$-\cup--\left|-\cup\cup-\left|\cup-\underline{\cup}\right.\right.$$
$$-\cup--\left|-\cup\cup-\left|\cup-\underline{\cup}\right.\right.$$
$$-\cup--\left|-\cup\cup-\left|\cup-\underline{\cup}\right.\right.$$
$$-\cup\cup-\left|\underline{\cup}\right.$$

7 Second archilochean
   1st line   hexameter
   2nd line $-\cup\cup\left|-\cup\cup\right|\underline{\cup}$